DESIGNED TO THRIVE

Reviews for *Designed to Thrive*

This book offers an excellent primer on how organizations can become self-correcting and future-ready. It demystifies systems thinking in a way that will appeal to various audiences – students, business and thought leaders, and policy makers.

Designed to Thrive successfully makes a compelling narrative: resilience arises from deliberate, well-informed design and monitoring of systems. Drawing on insights from science, philosophy, and business management, the author lays the foundation that system attributes of boundaries, interlinkages, and feedback loops apply universally across disciplines and are essential to understanding dynamics within a system and across various systems. Consequently, the complexities of real-world challenges (especially in a digital age) dictate a sustained attention to boundary conditions and how violating them can change the dynamic evolution of systems. In practical terms, the author concludes that organizations can better anticipate and survive shocks if they embrace the *CTS* framework of *Clarity* (on role and purpose), *Teamwork* (collaborative support networks), and *Systems* (effective fit-for-purpose linked processes).

Looking beyond the business world focus of the book, the text provides a bridging role for advancing resilience concepts and applications in engineering and biology, in explorations of control theory and sustainability science, and for organizational and community leaders interested in translating theoretical frameworks into actionable guides for "designing to thrive".

Designed to Thrive is timely and highly recommended as an essential read for all interested in resilience as the key to long-term sustainability.

Gene Leon, Ph.D.
Executive Director
Development Bank for Resilient Prosperity

Global appeal! As someone who has been employed in and remains involved in standardisation, I maintain that Dr Alison Gajadhar-Foster is a leading expert on quality infrastructure. Addressing systems and systems thinking from the perspective of the "soft side" of a quality infrastructure, is just brilliant. Seeing the big picture, as well as recognizing and managing connections are absolutely necessary for success, resilience and sustainability. If you accept this, then this book is a must read.

Betty Combie
Managing Director/Quality Management Consultant
Moz Inc

"A practical guide to not only understanding how systems function but what we can do to determine our own paths within. At its core, it's a prompt to be open eyed and inquisitive; a reminder to continually assess the direction envisaged; and to accept core inputs (feedback loops) - all which will ensure that we bring the best of ourselves to the fore, and importantly, that we not lose that best of ourselves to that space we entered.

Filled with easy to understand examples from an expert in systems dynamics, this is a worthwhile read and should be re-read, each time we enter a new environment, and or question our role and or the direction of the place we work. I do wish I had access to this insight earlier in my career. "

Anton E. Edmunds
Development practitioner, former diplomat, Caribbean citizen
General Manager, Country Department Caribbean Group,
Inter-American Development Bank

Dr. Gajadhar-Foster provides an insightful exploration into the principles and practice of systems thinking and resilience. She effectively uses real-world examples and personal experience to illustrate complex concepts, and make them accessible, relatable and implementable. She also provides a unique perspective, and practical framework, to encourage the reader to apply these concepts for their professional and personal benefit. From my perspective as an international expert working in developing and strengthening quality infrastructure in developing countries over many years, *Designed to Thrive* is a valuable resource for anyone looking to enhance their understanding of systems and practically apply the concepts to create resilient, sustainable systems in both their personal and professional lives.

Mike Peet PhD, MBA.
International Consultant

DESIGNED TO THRIVE

A Pathway to Building Resilient Systems

ALISON S. FOSTER, Ph.D.

Desgined to Thrive © Copyright 2025 KMA Consulting Services LLC

All rights reserved. No part of this publication may be reproduced, distributed or transmitted in any form or by any means, including photocopying, recording, or other electronic or mechanical methods, without the prior written permission of the publisher, except in the case of brief quotations embodied in critical reviews and certain other noncommercial uses permitted by copyright law.

Although the author and publisher have made every effort to ensure that the information in this book was correct at press time, the author and publisher do not assume and hereby disclaim any liability to any party for any loss, damage, or disruption caused by errors or omissions, whether such errors or omissions result from negligence, accident, or any other cause.

Adherence to all applicable laws and regulations, including international, federal, state and local governing professional licensing, business practices, advertising, and all other aspects of doing business in the US, Canada or any other jurisdiction is the sole responsibility of the reader and consumer.

Neither the author nor the publisher assumes any responsibility or liability whatsoever on behalf of the consumer or reader of this material. Any perceived slight of any individual or organisation is purely unintentional.

The resources in this book are provided for informational purposes only and should not be used to replace the specialised training and professional judgment of a health care or mental health care professional.

Neither the author nor the publisher can be held responsible for the use of the information provided within this book. Please always consult a trained professional before making any decision regarding treatment of yourself or others.

For more information, email alison@kma.consulting

ISBN: 979-8-9926054-0-2 - ebook
ISBN: 979-8-9926054-1-9 - paperback
ISBN: 979-8-9926054-2-6 - hardcover
ISBN: 979-8-9926054-3-3 - audiobook

To my soulmate Peter, and my precious gems, Koeba, Maquia, and Aleena, who are my greatest champions, and whose beautiful minds continue to inspire me.

"The use of systems thinking transcends many disciplines, supporting and connecting them in unintuitive but highly impactful ways".

—Ross D. Arnold and Jon P. Wade

Table of Contents

Forewords xiii
Chapter 1:   Welcome to the World of Organisations! 1

PART I: UNDERSTANDING SYSTEM DYNAMICS

Chapter 2:   What Really Is a System? 15
Chapter 3:   Identifying the System(s) You Are a Part Of 36
Chapter 4:   Understanding Relationships Within and
             Between Your System and Other Systems 48

PART II: DESIGNING THE SYSTEM YOU WANT TO BE A PART OF

Chapter 5:   Discovering the Processes That Exist Within Your System ... 63
Chapter 6:   Systems' Rules: Policies, Laws, Procedures,
             Standards, and Assumptions 77
Chapter 7:   Standardising the Processes That Work Well in
             Your System 88
Chapter 8:   Stabilising Your Standardised Processes 109

PART III: THE ART OF BUILDING RESILIENCE

Chapter 9:   What Does a Resilient System Look Like? 125
Chapter 10: A Strategy for Building Resilience: Lessons from a
             Personal Journey 137
Chapter 11: Thriving in a Complex World: The Journey Ahead 156

Acknowledgments 165
About the Author 166

FOREWORDS

The challenges faced by small island developing states (SIDS), and in particular the nations of the Organisation of Eastern Caribbean States (OECS), are as unique as they are complex. With limited natural resources, small economies vulnerable to external shocks, and the ever-present threats of climate change and natural disasters, our region exists in a state of continuous adaptation. The ability to build resilient systems, whether in governance, education, health, or economic development—has become not just an aspiration but an urgent necessity.

This book, *Designed to Thrive*, by Dr. Alison Gajadhar-Foster, is a timely and invaluable resource for all institutions, policymakers, and leaders, and particularly for those across the OECS and SIDS. It presents a structured yet practical approach to understanding and designing resilient systems that are adaptable, sustainable, and capable of long-term impact. And importantly, it is written in an accessible style that provides easy reading while explaining the scientific principles behind this paradigm. In a world increasingly defined by complexity and interdependence, this book provides the tools to navigate the shifting landscapes of governance, development, and organisational management.

ALISON S. FOSTER, Ph.D.

The Importance of Systems Thinking in SIDS

One of the defining characteristics of SIDS is their inherent interconnectedness. Unlike larger economies, where systems may function in isolation, in our small states, education, health, governance, economic activity, and environmental sustainability are all deeply intertwined. A disruption in one sector quickly reverberates through others.

For example, a climate-related disaster does not merely damage infrastructure, it affects livelihoods, education systems, healthcare, and national budgets. Similarly, economic shocks, whether from global market fluctuations or a downturn in tourism, impact every facet of our societies. This interconnectedness demands a new way of thinking—one that moves beyond short-term fixes and fragmented approaches toward holistic, systems-based solutions.

This book underscores the necessity of recognising relationships within and between systems. It highlights the importance of feedback loops in decision-making, demonstrating how institutions can anticipate challenges, mitigate risks, and design policies that enhance long-term stability. These principles align with the OECS's commitment to sustainable development, regional integration, and resilience-building.

Practical Applications for OECS Institutions

The insights provided in this book are not abstract theories; they are practical strategies that can be applied to improve governance, economic development, and institutional efficiency. Consider the following applications:

- **Governance and Policy Development:** By embedding systems thinking into policy design, governments can develop more coherent and adaptive strategies, ensuring that interventions in one sector do not create unintended consequences in another. This is critical for issues such as food security, climate adaptation, and economic diversification.
- **Resilient Infrastructure and Development:** Too often, infrastructure projects in the Caribbean focus solely on physical construction without the necessary governance and management frameworks. A systems-based approach ensures that investments in roads, buildings, and energy systems are integrated with policies that promote sustainability and disaster resilience.
- **Education Reform:** Education is a cornerstone of development, but traditional models often focus on isolated improvements rather than systemic transformation. This book provides a blueprint for reimagining education in a way that aligns with economic needs, technological advancements, and future workforce demands.
- **Economic and Environmental Resilience:** A thriving OECS economy must be built on systems that promote sustainability, equitable growth, and the responsible use of natural resources. This book's emphasis on system boundaries and adaptive strategies is particularly relevant for climate resilience, renewable energy development, and blue economy initiatives.

ALISON S. FOSTER, Ph.D.

The OECS Perspective: A Tool for Action

For the OECS and other SIDS, embracing systems thinking is no longer optional—it is imperative. Our unique vulnerabilities require us to think and act in ways that ensure long-term sustainability and regional prosperity. Whether in the public or the private sector, institutions across the Caribbean must adopt frameworks that account for complexity, interdependence, and resilience.

This book serves as a critical guide for leaders, policymakers, and practitioners who seek to make meaningful, lasting change. It provides a foundation for transforming how we govern, educate, build, and develop, ensuring that our nations are not merely surviving but thriving in the face of 21st-century challenges.

I commend the author for providing this much-needed resource and encourage all readers, especially those in leadership positions, to embrace the lessons contained within. It is my hope that this book will spark new conversations, inspire innovative policies, and serve as a blueprint for sustainable transformation in the OECS and beyond.

—Dr. Didacus P. Jules

As the Director General of the Organisation of Eastern Caribbean States (OECS) for over nine years, Dr. Jules leads the regional integration and cooperation agenda of ten member states and four associate members. He is responsible for the strategic direction, policy formulation, and operational management of the organisation, as well as the coordination of its relations with external partners and stakeholders.

****

I am delighted and honoured to write a forward for this book authored by my former very brilliant PhD mentee, Dr. Alison Gajadhar-Foster, who went on to be a major public and private sector servant of the Caribbean as well as an entrepreneur. The book is written in remarkably simple language that is readily accessible by any reader with a modest mastery of English and is coloured and enlivened by pertinent experiential examples.

Alison and I spent her PhD days building systems of some metal ions and exploring communication within and between them, using laser beams. Metal ion systems are visible, but the forces holding them together and those controlling or facilitating their communications are not. Alison explored, understood, and clearly explained the critical features of those metal ion assemblies and their influence on communication mechanisms between and within them. It is fascinating to see in this book how this skill has been successfully adapted to interrogating, explaining, and communicating intricate behaviours of diverse personal and organisational systems.

This book's clever use of vocabulary connecting phenomena in the realms of physical and social sciences successfully establishes a continuum between natural and social systems. The clarity so obtained drives home the nature of forces that hold systems together and how the human brain responds to them; reveals opportunities for manipulating them to enhance their utility; and demonstrates the effectiveness of quality infrastructures as guardrails enhancing trust and resilience in systems.

The first part of the book explores what systems are and makes a good case for systems thinking and associated dynamics. The

ALISON S. FOSTER, Ph.D.

second part challenges the reader to design the desired personal or organisational systems with the benefit of in-depth understanding of embedded processes (core and supporting), guardrails (or rules), and feeder loops (which could enforce or derail the system's success and sustainability). The final part explores resilience in systems, how to build it and, thereby, thrive as an individual or organisation in a complex world.

The book is a required reading for individuals and organisations seeking to achieve profitability, growth, and institutional success and resilience; students of human and organisational behaviour; and political and church leaders/members (especially in developing countries) seeking to build cohesive communities focused on personal, community, or national development and sustainability. The book is also a highly recommended reading for anybody who enjoys insightful immersion in complex phenomena.

—Professor Ishenkumba A. Kahwa

Ishenkumba A. Kahwa is Emeritus Professor of Chemistry at the University of the West Indies, Mona Campus where he served as Head of Department of Chemistry; Dean Faculty of Science and Technology; Deputy Principal; and Programme Development Leader for Occupational and Environmental Safety and Health. Professor Kahwa also chairs and serves as a member of several boards of directors.

CHAPTER 1

Welcome to the World of Organisations!

Our separateness is a delusion of our consciousness.
—**Albert Einstein**

"Welcome to the organisation! Fasten your seatbelt … it's going to be a bumpy ride. You may not get to the destination intended, but we guarantee—you will remain within the universe! Once you have the entire prism of your being here, with all its personal dimensions, you're sure to enjoy the ride!"

"But no! I must be in the wrong place. I'm not part of an organisation!"

"I didn't sign up for this. I'm not a CEO—I'm a doctor".

"Neither did I—I'm a lawyer".

"I'm an innovator—an entrepreneur".

"But what about me? I'm just a mom and a wife!"

"Calm down. You all belong here. You all are part of a system. Really, you are part of multiple systems. Once you recognise this and identify those systems, you'll be in a much better position to steer your system, and your life, and enact positive change when problems arise. But you first need to believe you can!"

*

Then the phone rang, interrupting the vivid and revelatory dream I was having. It was the wee hours of the morning, so when I heard my father's voice on the line, my heart raced.

At the time, I was in England, starting off a post doctorial fellowship programme. During all my years away from my homeland, Saint Lucia, my father had never initiated a call to me—unless something was wrong. This was due simply to his reserved personality. I knew he cared tremendously about me. Even so, he was never one to initiate small talk, unless he felt he had something important to say—and boy, then he would talk!

As my heart skipped a beat, without asking me how I was doing, he went straight to point, "There's a job for you at home".

My bewilderment only deepened at that point. "What? A job for me?"

At that juncture in my life, I had been steeped in pure and applied chemistry for over seven years. With the help of the academics I was surrounded by, who constantly prodded me, I had become convinced that there was nothing for me back on the small island nation I called home. At least nothing that would keep that fire burning in me, which radiated as a glow through my eyes. At that time, all I needed was to walk into a laboratory, surrounded by beakers and test tubes, and any talk about atomic behaviour, molecules, and reactions would light me up. I dreamed and breathed chemistry.

Perhaps it was the audacious confidence my father demonstrated in me or the rare prospect of landing a decent job on Saint Lucia other than teaching (which seemed to be the resting place for most who returned home with a pure science background), coupled with my then unacknowledged personal ambitions of starting a family back home … whatever it was, I instinctively jumped to the challenge. Little did I know what that challenge really was.

It was at that point, my journey into a career underpinned by the tenets of systems and systems thinking began. At the core of my professional experience has been standardisation and quality-related matters, working within the governance, management, and operational space. Later, after several years working within the public sector and manufacturing industry, as well as briefly in the legislature, my professional journey morphed into consulting services, through my company, KMA Consulting Ltd (www.kma.consulting).

It took several years of homemaking, raising children, building and breaking relationships, and leading several projects and improvement initiatives for me to come to the realisation that the principles governing all these facets of life are really the same. Indeed, these principles all draw on the same core that lies at the heart of nature and natural science. A core subject matter, which, for the purpose of this book, I will refer to as "systems theory". KMA has, therefore, given me a vehicle through which I can give back and help leaders, managers, and operators within organisational systems benefit from the lessons I have learnt by not repeating some of the mistakes that I have made in areas related to business, organisational development, and policy development and implementation. Through KMA, I have helped organisations solve complex problems, whether through strategy formulation and policy development or implementing measures to make their operations more efficient and effective. In all instances, my greatest joy has been witnessing my clients' joy when a problem has been solved.

Why Systems and Systems Thinking

In a world where success appears to be defined by how well you can harness the power of information technology including artificial intelligence, the role of the human being and the degree of human-centeredness are becoming increasingly important for the survival of our man-made systems. Yet, in a recent survey conducted by the International Organization for Standardization (ISO) Technical Committee on Information Security, only about 10% of respondents attributed information security risks to humans. Notwithstanding these results, the IT security experts confirm that all major information security breaches occur as a result of human error. These surveys are completed by humans, so what is it that prevents us humans from acknowledging and accepting the role of the person, the role of the human being, when errors occur within a system?

This has been puzzling to me, and it has become even more so since the COVID-19 pandemic, amidst the accelerated rate of climate change and developments in technology. Indeed, we have entered a new industrialisation era, which highlights the need to focus on the human being in all the policies we develop and implement to grow our social economy. In this modern era of personalisation, where the focus is now on designing products and systems to suit individual needs, it is ironic that we have yet to find a truly successful way to allow humans to work together effectively and efficiently to build resilient systems.

I strongly believe this is because we have not been able to master the art of applying systems thinking successfully when it comes to building resilient human systems. For instance, this deficiency in a systems approach and systems thinking has often led to disastrous outcomes from improvement initiatives concentrated on systemisation. In excess of 2.5 decades, functioning as an entrepreneur, director, chief executive officer, manager, parliamentarian, and consultant, I have witnessed too much money being thrown down the drain, with the aim of helping organisations grow and access new markets. Very often, these efforts have been focused on assisting organisations to systemise activities based on rules or standards that are not applicable to the context in which their system operates. This error is amplified, as it is driven primarily by a need to satisfy demands from buyers and regulators in jurisdictions totally different to the one in which the business entity or organisation operates.

Further, too often entities are bullied into systemising processes that have not been piloted or tested within their systems first to determine whether the rules or standards that are handed down to them can work to the benefit of the system's owner stakeholders and other interested parties. It is a consequence of experiencing this agony personally and intimately witnessing the pain of other entrepreneurs and leaders of organisational systems whom I have assisted in the past, that has propelled me to write this book.

A Systems World

Having had the privilege of interacting with so many brilliant people, at all levels within society, I often wonder why we find it difficult to adopt a systems approach to solving problems, particularly in the developing world. Perhaps it is because our focus for building resilience has been misguided. Too often the focus has been placed on constructing a building, a road, or some other concrete thing. Instead, I believe we should be focusing our efforts on building resilience in something we cannot feel or touch. If the focus for building resilience continues to only be on a road, bridge, or building, this is going against what nature has taught us. Nature has taught us that the object for building resilience ought not to be a focus on only one thing.

The real object for resilience building in its totality is impossible to touch or hold. This is because that object of focus ought to be a system. While some elements within the system can be perceived through the human being's five senses of touch, sight, hearing, taste, and smell, many other elements in their purest and basic form cannot be observed and perceived. Incidentally, the elements that fall into this category form the core of the system and will be described as energy throughout this book.

Systems exist, regardless of whether we possess the ability to think in systems. And that dream from which I was awoken on that night in February of 1999, the dream described at the start of this chapter, later turned out to be an epiphany for me. Let me explain.

When we can think in systems, we develop an ability to understand, analyse, and interact more effectively with the systems we are a part of and those we are surrounded by. Moreover, in a systems world, there is no barrier between science, arts, and business disciplines. And contrary to what academia teaches, in a practical systems world, complex problems are solved in a multi-faceted manner, drawing on all disciplines necessary to solve the problem.

Before we go further in this book, it is necessary to establish a common understanding of some terms that will be used repeatedly. Using the diagram below, I have attempted to differentiate the various types of systems that exist within our world. The diagram provides a pictorial view of the dichotomy of systems, how the different types of systems that are referred to within this book are grouped together, and their relationship with each other. Some definitions are embedded into the diagram to assist you in understanding the logic used to group these various systems. This logic is based on a number of factors, the main one being focused on the system's purpose and how it is treated.

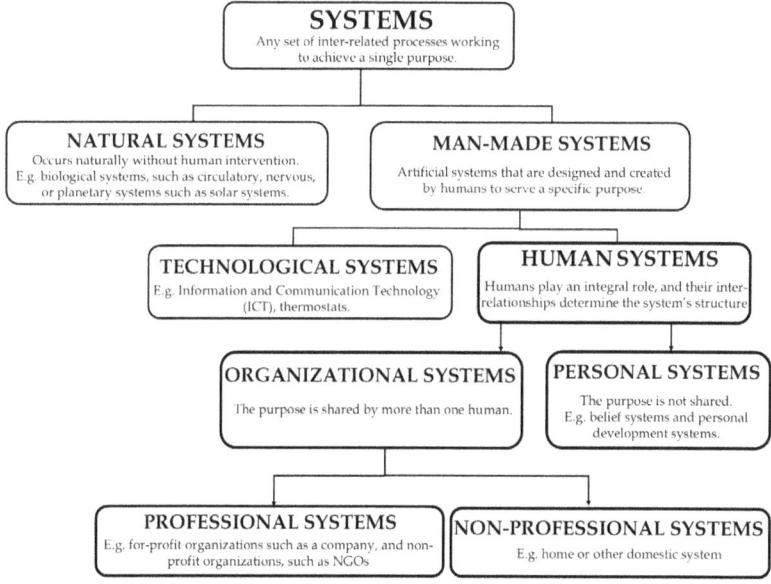

Note that an organisational system can be of any type—profit, non-profit, or even a household—and that this definition is consistent with the one used by the International Organization for Standardization (ISO), which states that an organisation refers to any group of people coming together for a common cause or purpose.

More importantly, is the understanding that an organisational system is made up of multiple systems. This type of system therefore offers a perfect example of what is often referred to as 'systems-in-systems'. The diagram below demonstrates the connectivity of all sub-systems within a business organizational system, working together in harmony to achieve the single purpose of the overall organizational system, - which is to deliver value to its customers through the products and/or services it produces.

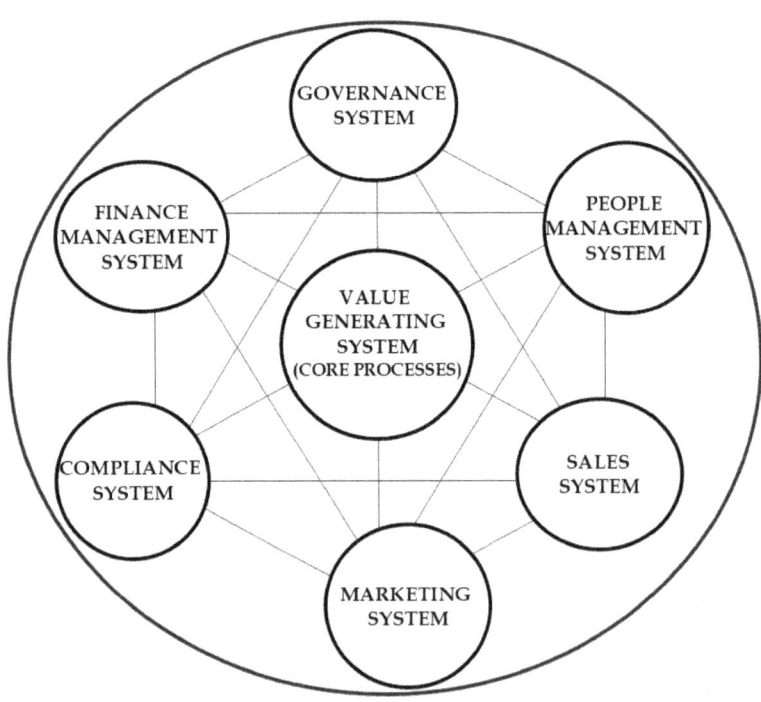

This Book's Promise

As humans, we are limited by our cognitive ability to think in linear and logical patterns. But systems are not naturally made up of linear patterns. They are made up of multi-dimensional structures or frameworks. It is, therefore, not surprising that thinking in systems may often not come naturally to us, unless we train our brains to think in this way. Developing this skillset could be particularly challenging for those of us who have been cultured in an environment that is characterised by a history of enslavement and colonisation, as is true for me and others who have grown up in small island developing states like Saint Lucia. Perhaps this is because our ancestors had not traditionally been involved in conscious efforts to shape their futures. Such efforts involve embracing the "view from the top"—a view that is beyond the individual parts of the system. This view can only be gained at a higher altitude, which is the only level at which a system, its boundaries, and the interdependence of its processes can be appreciated.

I believe that for those of us growing up in such an environment, our DNA/coding has been so influenced by acts of "doing" at lower altitudes, and "doing as we have been told", that the evolution of our brains has been biased against developing an inherent capacity to embrace holism and to employ a systems approach to solving problems. Notwithstanding, there is evidence of an absence of systems thinking in the world as a whole, not just in developing countries. Many would agree that there is no shortage of examples, not just within the Caribbean, of development blunders related to hard infrastructure, such as roads and buildings, that we are often gifted or made highly indebted for.

Such hard infrastructure often remains useless because of a lack of a systems approach to development, by, among other things, failing to incorporate the appropriate "soft" infrastructure, such as robust governance and management systems. Too often, we are so blindsided in the resources needed for the invisible "soft" infrastructure that our actions are driven by a magical belief that governance and management processes will take place on their own, requiring no resources at all.

I am aware that research has shown that a focus only on the perceptual whole (the system) can reduce our conscious ability to focus on the system's parts—something which is equally important. This limitation can, in fact, be disastrous for problem-solving, which is crucial to building resilient systems. This book will, therefore, help you to not only identify and define the systems that you are a part of, but it will also help you design and create the systems you want to be in and to be responsible for, and importantly, it will teach you how to think in systems effectively. This book will also help you understand how to use analytical skills to reduce your systems into simpler, smaller parts in order to facilitate a better understanding of your system, predict its behaviour, and devise modifications to produce the desired results from the system.

My hope is that by reading this book you will have an opportunity to transform your thinking and mindset, and obtain the necessary skillset to help you design, develop, direct, control, and sustain any "thing" or organisation you want to, especially in an environment of limited resources. The principles for building, sustaining, and growing systems are the same, irrespective of the technical domain the system is operating in, whether or not the system is natural or man-made, or operating within a personal or organisational context. These principles will be explained throughout the ensuing chapters within this book.

It is my hope that by the end of this book, you will be equipped with a pathway that you can adapt and utilise to assist you to design, build, and maintain a resilient system. A system that has the ability to sustain itself by effectively connecting all its sub-systems (networking silos), embracing technology, especially artificial intelligence, and thriving through any type of man-made or natural disaster brought on by climate change, pandemics, political blunders, or other events.

The Book's Approach

This book, unlike many other systems-related books, adopts a human systems approach to dealing with man-made systems, by, among other things, demonstrating the intrinsic link or interdependence between personal systems and organisational systems.

To do so, the book is structured into three main parts: the first part focuses on gaining a deeper understanding of what a system really is and how to identify the actual system(s) you are a part of.

The second part of this book focuses on techniques to create the system(s) you want and how to make that system (or those systems) produce the results you want.

Finally, the last part of the book focuses on designing for and building resilience into your system(s).

After reading this book, you will be better able to appreciate that growth over a specified period does not necessarily equate to resilience. In fact, uncontrolled growth, like cancer, often leads to system failure, which, if left unchecked, all systems can do. A resilient system, however, always demonstrates a remarkable ability to restructure itself and thrive over time. I have, therefore, taken much care to differentiate and separate the two objectives—growth and resilience—as I believe that these two aims are often mistakenly entwined, especially in the developing world's context, where public governance systems are often driven by short-term political gains within a democratic context.

By the end of the book, it is my hope that you will be convinced that survival and prosperity in this new era necessitates viewing the world through a systems lens, and this requires building the human capacity to think in systems. My views on systems and systems thinking are not only based on peer-reviewed published research papers, but also on my own experiential learning—the failures and successes I have made over the years, in both my professional and personal life. I have attempted to express these thoughts in the least complex and technical way possible, deliberately omitting mathematical or scientific formulae, with the hope that you too may be able to apply these principles in a useful manner to your life.

Happy reading!

PART I

UNDERSTANDING SYSTEM DYNAMICS

CHAPTER 2

What Really Is a System?

Ever since the Industrial Revolution, Western society had benefitted from science, logic, and reductionism over intuition and holism.
—**Donella H. Meadows**

There is no denying the growing attention being given to systems theory and systems thinking in this increasingly globalised and digitised world order. This trend is occurring notwithstanding the lag in the development of our education system, which continues to be steeped in its traditional mode, narrowly focusing on a reductionist methodology for teaching many disciplines, including the sciences. Reductionism, which narrowly focuses on only parts of a system, has its benefits for breaking down complex problems. But every so often, with this approach, learners lose an opportunity to appreciate the importance of understanding the relevance of the context of the problem, and the impact of the problem's context on finding a suitable solution.

In addition, reductionist methods of teaching focus too much on linear approaches to problem-solving, such as deduction, logic, and root cause analysis. This is problematic because we know that usually problems within organisations are systemic and require a holistic, multi-dimensional approach to problem-solving. While the reductionist approach to learning is needed to understand systems dynamics through simplification, this approach, I believe, has unintentionally been responsible for our continued compulsion to manage our personal lives and organisations with a bounded rationality, focusing on only the parts within our proximity, rather than the extended whole. It is, therefore, time that we integrate teaching methodologies into our learning systems that focus on the "big picture", solving problems through a lens of systems thinking.

I am heartened that with the global focus on sustainable development, the overemphasis on the reductionist approach will soon be a thing of the past. The need to pay attention to the whole, and not just its individual parts, has gained tremendous traction over the past few decades. Holism, and the body of knowledge surrounding systems thinking focuses on the behaviour of complex wholes. This knowledge is predicated on the fact that the properties of the whole are much greater than, and indeed different from, the sum of the whole's individual parts. Yes, while "one plus one equals two" is a rule that holds for mathematical and other reductionist scientific methodologies, this rule does not apply to systems science and systems thinking, which lie at the heart of holism.

A Brief Background to Systems Thinking

Contrary to popular belief, the importance of systems thinking to the survival of our human systems did not begin with the proclamation of the United Nations Sustainable Development Goals in 2015. From the biblical era, there is evidence of an appreciation of systems theory, which include phenomena associated with reinforcing feedback loops. Feedback loops are a critical feature of systems, particularly in determining the outcome of a system's processes. You will learn more about feedback loops and their role in determining the outcome of processes within systems later in this chapter.

But for now, consider an example from the biblical era, reflected in a verse in one of the four canonical gospels in the New Testament of the Christian Bible, the Gospel of Mark, where Mark, the Evangelist, writes: "For he that hath, to him shall be given; and he that hath not, from him shall be taken" (Mark 4:25). I like this verse, because it speaks directly to a concept used in personal systems, such as your belief system, in relation to the notion of "abundance". Now it is well established by the psychological sciences that if your belief system is aligned and filled with one of abundance, the feedback loop that is created with the universe is one that brings you more abundance. Alternatively, if your belief system is characterised by one of lacking or scarcity, the feedback, or reinforcing loop will be one of scarcity.

Approaching a bit to our lifetime, in the modern era, from as far back as 1945, seminal work on General Systems Theory (GST) was published by Austrian scientist Ludwig von Bertalanffy, followed by the published work of philosopher and systems scientist, C. West Churchman, who made significant contributions to the fields of systems theory and management science between the 1940s and the 1970s. Other early notable contributions to this body of knowledge emanate from the Massachusetts Institute of Technology's team of scientists such as Jay Forrester, Donella Meadows, and Peter Senge within the period 1950 to 2000. Additionally, Canadian-born political scientist, David Easton, applied systems theory to behavourial research in politics, during the second half of the 20th century. These individuals and many others contributed significantly to the rich tapestry of systems thinking, demonstrating its relevance and application across a variety of cultural and disciplinary contexts, particularly in management sciences.

More importantly, efforts by these individuals and globally recognised organisations, such as those within the United Nations system, all highlight the universal value and adaptability of systems thinking principles to address complex problems worldwide. Now, the important role of systems and systems thinking is so well established that since the 1980s, the International Organization for Standardization (ISO) has rooted all its management systems standards in system philosophy, influenced heavily by the work of the renowned quality control and improvement gurus, Walter A. Shewhart and Edward W. Deming.

Understanding Systems

As you saw earlier, systems occur both naturally and man-made, and in all forms. There are systems on various scales, creating systems within systems, within systems. For instance, the entire universe is a system, but it comprises trillions of smaller systems, such as galaxies, solar systems, planets, continents, countries, cities, communities, and households. Likewise, within the household, the human body is a system, comprising several systems such as your digestive system, respiratory system, coronary system, and belief system.

Any man-made system can be created by humans to serve a specific purpose that the humans created it for. Within man-made systems, there are also sub-systems, such as the man-made system of an organisation, with its sub-systems, such as finance, human resources, and marketing. Sub-systems are important to make it easier to manage the entire system. The problem that arises much too often occurs when the sub-systems operate as silos, with the inability to network properly. In subsequent chapters we will expand on how man-made systems can be designed and created for growth and resilience, using the same principles of naturally occurring resilient systems, which rely on controlled interactions for effective networking.

But first, we must establish a common understanding of what we really mean when we describe something as being a system. It is necessary to develop the skills needed to first identify whether or not a system actually exists, and if it does, what it is, before rushing to apply policies and other rules, associated with system dynamics. Too often, especially in the developing world context, I have seen a rush to apply rules, without first taking the time to understand what the system is.

A scan of the literature would reveal that there are several definitions for a "system" in use throughout academia and across various scientific disciplines. However, the one offered by environmental scientist, educator, and writer Donella H. Meadows is most appealing to me, because of its simplicity. So, for the purpose of this book, I will use the following adaptation of Dr. Meadows' definition: "A system is a set of elements interconnected in such a way that they produce their own pattern of behaviour over time". With this definition, it is easy to deduce that a system must have the following four basic components in order to exist, even if it is for a fleeting moment or short time:

1. **Elements:** These are the parts of the system. These parts could be tangible, such as the parts or organs that make up your digestive system—mouth, trachea, stomach, and intestines—or the buildings housing hospitals and health centres within a public health system.

Alternatively, and always occurring in combination with the intangibles, there are elements within the system that are intangible, that is, they cannot be touched, heard, or seen by the naked eye; however, they exist, nonetheless. These can be described by energy and form part of all processes within a system, such as decision-making processes within a business management system, a household, or any other organisation; chemical reactions within a catalytic or acid-base system; or photons within a lighting system.

For descriptive simplicity, the mechanics of all systems can be broken down into its processes. The elements in relation to the system's processes include inputs, resources, and outputs or products. In systems lingo, the term "stock" is also used to refer to any pool of resources or output of a system. This could be tangible, like the volume of water in a tank, or intangible, like the level of stress in a household or other organisation.

2. **Structure/Interconnections:** A system must have a structure. This structure serves as the backbone on which the system exists and is supported by. As we will see later, the system's structure plays a crucial role in its survival, and the strength of its structure determines whether the system survives, thrives, or dies. The system's structure, however, is not visible to the naked eye, but it can be described by the way in which the system's parts interact with one another. In other words, the system's structure is determined by the relationship between the elements within the system. These interactions take place via an exchange of information.

All information is exchanged via the transfer of energy or electromagnetic radiation. Humans have developed the capacity to code this information transferred through energy into language or signals, which could be interpreted by the human brain. However, in the absence of the interpretation machine, the human brain, coded or uncoded information in its basic form is really the same: packets of energy. In chemistry, we study the transfer of this energy at the sub-atomic, atomic, and molecular levels. All energy is made up of quanta, which is the plural term for the minimum amount of physical entity involved in the interaction ("quantum" is the singular term). In the context of electromagnetic radiation like light, a quantum refers to the minimum amount of energy that can be transported, known as a photon.

All elements or matter are made up of atoms, and atoms can only absorb or release discrete packets of energy, or quanta. Consequently, at atomic and molecular levels, particles exhibit behaviour that can only be explained by quantum mechanics. The principles of quantum mechanics, as well as thermodynamics, are foundational to understanding how energy and matter interact, and consequently, to an understanding of how systems behave. Later, as we delve deeper into the behaviour patterns of systems, the basic aspects of these, the body of knowledge associated with quantum mechanics and thermodynamics, and their applicability to building resilient systems will become clearer.

3. **Purpose/Function:** A system must have a purpose. Without a purpose, a system cannot exist. For non-human systems, such as IT systems or chemical reactions, the term "function" is usually used instead of "purpose". However, since all systems within our daily lives comprise both human and non-human elements, all systems have a purpose. So important is the purpose to the existence of the system, that the system is typically named or described by its purpose—such as your respiratory system, a wastewater management system, or an organisation's governance system.

4. **Boundaries:** The humans within the system need mechanisms to ensure that the system is continuously meeting its purpose. To assist them in doing so, imaginary boundaries are created to facilitate the governance, management, and operation of the system. Sometimes, these boundaries may have physical or tangible artifacts to ease understanding where they exist. An example would be a political system or country with borders.

To help you understand how these four components are demonstrated within a real system, let us use an organisational system, such as a public hospital. The boundaries of that organisation would be influenced by its purpose—the reason it was established. For example, if it was established to serve the health needs of the population of a particular community, its boundary would be defined by this. This organisation would have different sub-systems, for governance, management, and operations, each with its own boundaries within the overall organisational system. The hospital will have employees, such as doctors, nurses, pharmacists, orderlies, accountants, etc. These employees, together with the medical equipment, standard operating procedures, drugs and other inputs, serve as the elements within the system. The boundaries, together with the interactions between the humans within the system, which is often reflected by the system's organisational chart, establishes the structure of the system. Elements related to energy, or information, flow through the structure of the system.

Now that you know the four basic components of a system, it is important to understand the core behaviour patterns of the system. Understanding the organic behaviour of systems is important to enable you to recognise when a system exists, what system you are a part of, and what system you want to create.

There is a plethora of scientific data, literature, and on-going research dedicated to understanding the behaviour of systems. However, in this book, I will expand on two key features of a system that I believe must be understood and appreciated, in order to apply systems thinking effectively and to steer and control any system you desire. These two features are feedback loops and dynamism.

Feedback Loops

We saw earlier that one of the four core components of a system is its structure, which is determined by the interactions and relationships between a system's elements. A system is made up of both linear relationships, known as flows, and non-linear relationships. Linear relationships are easier to understand, as they progress in one direction, making it simple to be depicted as a flow from left to right, with inputs being transformed into outputs, or top-down, describing how coded information flows. A common example of a linear relationship would be depicted by a process flowchart, describing the steps or activities to be taken within a process. See the figure below to see an example of linear relationships in a system; in this case, it is a system that describes the process for cooking rice:

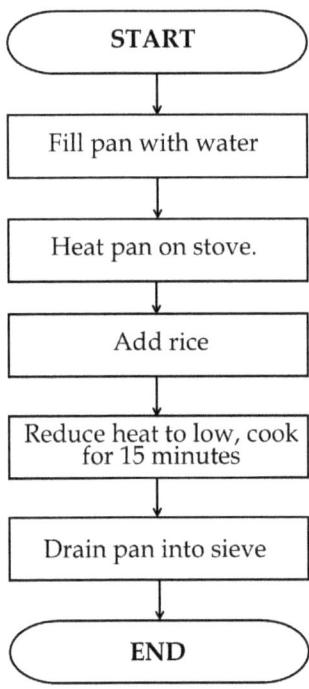

The other type of relationship between the system's elements is non-linear in nature. These types of relationships are critical, as they determine the overall behaviour and outcome of the system. One such important type of non-linear relationship is known as a feedback loop, which is a closed chain of causal connections within the system. For simplicity, the following figure demonstrates what a non-linear relation could look like when a feedback loop is inserted into a linear relationship, such as the same linear process to cook rice:

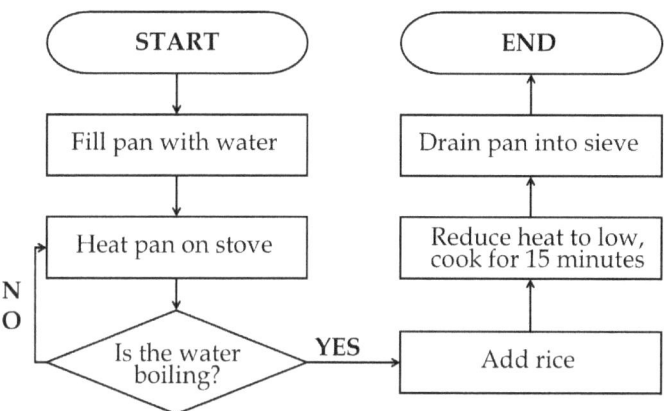

In the above diagram, the feedback loop occurs as a result of an observer or temperature sensor determining whether the water is boiling. If yes, the operator, i.e., the person cooking the rice, can proceed to add the rice. If no, the operator allows the pan with the water to continue to be heated. In this instance, the temperature of the water is serving as an indicator, and the response to the temperature measurement or observation (if bubbles are being observed to be generated from the bottom of the pan) would determine the next activity, meaning which direction the process flows.

Process maps are the best attempt to reflect non-linear relationships, but these maps demonstrate the connections only in a two-dimensional fashion on paper or on a screen. As if these diagrams are not complex enough, non-linear relationships are even more complex, as they occur in a multitude of directions. Unlike a system's linear relationships, its non-linear relationships, such as feedback loops, are often complex because of their multi-dimensional nature, with the capacity to deliver coded and uncoded information to various processes within the system.

Although we will expand on this later, at this point, it is just necessary for you to know that by "coded" information, I refer to information that is documented in a manner that can be stored, accessed, retrieved, transferred, transported, and destroyed. Examples of coded information could be in information in a printed format, such as manuals and handbooks. But coded information could be solely digitised, such as video or voice recordings. For instance, if we were to continue to use the above example of cooking rice, the measurements taken for the temperature indicator could be recorded on a chart. Once recorded, this could serve as documented or coded information. "Uncoded" information, on the other hand, has no language attached to it, and it is difficult to be transferred and transported in a standardised manner. As we will see in a later chapter, an example of this would be your assumptions. In the cooking of rice example above, uncoded information could be the operator's (or cook's) impression that the water is boiling, which then moves them to proceed to add the rice.

The elements within the system will respond to the information delivered through the system's feedback loops. It is, therefore, reasonable to surmise that the information received in a feedback loop will determine the behaviour and resilience of the system. There are several examples in both natural and man-made systems of multi-dimensional relationships, such as feedback loops at work. A classic example of this at work in a man-made non-human system is the thermostat, used for air-conditioning and heating systems in buildings. When the sensor senses that the temperature drops below a set point, the heater is turned on to increase the temperature of the environment. Likewise, if the sensor detects that the temperature in the environment has increased to a value above the set point, this will trigger the cooling system to be turned on, to cool the environment.

Feedback loops operating within human organisational systems are usually much more complex than this though. This is because all human organisational systems involve personal sub-systems, belonging to all the individual humans working within the human organisational system. Every individual receives and interprets the information they receive in a subjective manner, which is influenced by many factors, including the individual's personal experience. The way in which humans within a human organisational system interpret information received by the system is at the core of managing the quality of the system. This is why a carefully designed and executed quality management system is a critical sub-system of any organisational system desirous of achieving sustainability.

To help you understand the complexity of feedback loops operating within human systems, I think it is necessary to explain the relationship between quality and qualia, a key attribute of the human brain.

The Role of Quality and Qualia in Assessing Information Received through Feedback Loops

At this point in the evolution of our existence, it is challenging for the human brain to visualise and understand physical concepts in multi-dimensional models, which is how systems naturally exist. Because of this limitation, an appreciation of the role of quality and qualia in the delivery and interpretation of information received through feedback loops in human systems is crucial, in order to steer and control your system effectively.

"Quality" is used to describe measurable characteristics or attributes of seen and unseen matter, including energy. The quality of matter can be given descriptive features, such as shape, colour, odour, or texture. The description of the quality of a product, tangible or intangible, is often used to distinguish products or process outputs from each other. The output's quality is determined by the level of control of the linear relationships between the system's elements. These linear relationships could be managed using reductionist methods, such as statistical process control (SPC) methods, and other tried and proven scientific tools and techniques. Statisticians and quality managers are versed in these methods, but it is important for anyone who is responsible for the performance of a system to have a basic understanding of SPC. While there is quite a lot of information on SPC techniques and methods available in published books and on the internet, you will get a better general understanding of the principles of these methods in the second part of this book, when we delve deeper into techniques for designing the system you want.

Although quality and qualia share a linguistic origin, unlike quality, which refers to properties of the object, the word "qualia" explains the human perspective, and is rooted in philosophy and the cognitive sciences. Qualia are therefore subjective, individual experiences of perceptions of the quality of matter. Qualia are private and unique only to the person experiencing it. A subjective experience arises from an individual's interaction with the quality of matter. This experience is heavily influenced by the individual's unique frame of reference, or mindset. For example, take the colour blue. The quality of light wavelength to make the colour blue is measurable and objective, but the qualia of seeing the colour blue is personal and subjective, as the stimulus or information in the form of energy passes through the human brain—the human being's interpretation machine.

Quality refers to the extent to which the products produced by the system's processes meet established parameters or standards.

Therefore, sub-systems, such as quality management systems, could be architectured and implemented in a manner to control the quality of the products produced by the system in the least subjective manner. Some of this will be discussed later.

The tricky aspect of managing the quality of the overall organisational system, however, is due to the relationship between quality and the more subjective influence of qualia in the personal system. To control the subjective impact of qualia on quality, it is important that the system's feedback loops be controlled. This is achieved by controlling the structure of the system, which is a function of the interactions within the system. To do so effectively requires the application of a skillset associated with systems thinking. In the final part of this book, you will learn how to develop this skillset.

Timing and Feedback Loops

It is also important to note that the system does not receive information through its feedback loops in real time. There is always a lag in the time taken for the information to be transferred through the system's structure. Consequently, information received via feedback loops can only be used to influence the system's future behaviour or the system's response to activities done in the past. As will be shown later in the book, understanding this delay period, and leveraging it, is a critical aspect of managing the system through effective strategy development and robust planning.

Dynamism

At the sub-atomic, atomic, and molecular levels, interactions between elements within the system are in constant motion, moving back and forth. At the macroscopic level, this may not be obvious to the human brain. Although the make-up of our brain favours the perception of stability, in all systems, both natural and man-made, no process is static. In reality, the perceived stability of a system simply implies that its processes have reached a state of equilibrium —with its flows oscillating back and forth at an equal rate. If the sum and rate of inflows exceed the sum and rate of outflows, the system's stock level will rise. Likewise, if the sum and rate of outflows exceed the sum and rate of inflows, its stock level will fall. For example, in a water system with a reservoir of water as its stock, if the rate of flow of water out of the reservoir is faster than the rate of flow of water into it, the level, or the volume of water within the reservoir, will be depleted. If water is flowing outside of the reservoir at a slower rate compared to the rate it is entering the reservoir, the water stock level will increase. Likewise, if the rate of flow of water leaving the reservoir equals the rate of flow entering it, then the volume of water in the reservoir will appear to be stable.

The above example demonstrates the behaviour of all systems, in that there is always a constant flow of energy, stock, or elements within the system's processes and between systems. This concept is expanded in the second part of the book. At this point, it is important just to understand that when thinking in systems, stability is perceived only when equilibrium is achieved between and within all the processes within the system. This is sometimes referred to as dynamic equilibrium, and, at the systems level, occurs only when the sum and rate of outflows from the system equals the sum and rate of inflows into the system.

The way in which the non-linear interconnections or interactions combine into feedback loops is a key factor that influences the dynamic behaviour of the system because, as we saw earlier, a system's processes always respond to the information received via its feedback loops. Systems with similar feedback structures demonstrate similar dynamic behaviour patterns. This is an important factor to consider if you are embarking on exercises related to benchmarking and self-assessment based on maturity models to help you improve your organisational system's performance. Again, much more will be said on this later in the book.

System Stability

While identifying and understanding non-linear relationships like feedback loops is the key to understanding the behaviour of the system, there are a few points to note about achieving stability, which is the same as achieving a state of equilibrium in natural systems. A state of equilibrium is the goal sought by all natural systems, just as stability is the goal sought by all man-made systems. This is consistent with the natural laws of thermodynamics, which, from a scientific point of view, explain the behaviour of all systems. The second law of thermodynamics states that all processes will tend to move towards a state of maximum entropy or chaos. Entropy is a measure of disorder/chaos or randomness in the system, and it is central to thermodynamics. When processes are in a state of equilibrium, they are at their maximum entropy level. In this state of maximum disorder, there is less energy to do work, and more information is needed to understand the system. The converse is true. If you want to have more energy available in your system to do the work you want and to make it simpler for you to understand what is going on in your system, you will want to control the level of chaos by lowering the entropy level in your system. In man-made systems, this can only be achieved by establishing appropriate control or compliance sub-systems within your organisational system. The role of these systems will be expounded on later in this book.

Be careful, however, not to allow the perceived stability of your system to cause you to believe that it is stable. You can only take some level of comfort in your system's stability if this stability is supported by appropriate feedback loops, which are balancing and equilibrating the system. If you do not have effective feedback loops within your system, then your perception of stability may just be due to a delay in the transmission of information to your system's processes. If this is the case, your system will be exposed to a high risk of drastic failure because when it does receive the feedback information, which it will at some point, it may respond in an uncontrollable manner, often with severe undesirable consequences.

The collapse of the Enron Corporation, a once innovative US company specialising in energy trading, derivatives, and broadband service, at the turn of the 21st century, remains one of the most infamous scandals in the history of corporate organisational systems. This scandal serves as a cautionary example of the consequences of a system not receiving accurate information in a timely manner. Measures were used by the head of the organisation's financial system to hide its debt and inflate its profits by using special purpose entities (SPEs) to move liabilities off the company's balance sheet. In doing so, the company was perceived to be financially stable by its investors and shareholders.

The feedback loop, which was established to provide the organisation's governing body with timely information, was also compromised by facilitation from its financial auditors. This false perception of financial stability continued for five years, until accurate information was exposed, causing the company to be forced into bankruptcy in December of 2001. Markets crashed as the value of shares plummeted, creating a ripple effect in several sectors, including the housing market. Hundreds of people lost jobs and their life savings in the aftermath, as overnight, the value of shares in Enron plunged from $99 to less than $1, when the true information regarding its financial health was exposed. During the period of five years, when shareholders and directors were not receiving the correct information to guide their decision-making, the institution continued along the destructive path, maintaining the self-defeating behaviour of its executives, and investors continued to invest, which ultimately led to an increase in the magnitude of their loss. If the correct information about the financial health of the organisation had been presented to the organisation's decision-makers in a timely manner, actions could have been taken to avert the destruction of the company and reduce the magnitude of the concomitant losses.

The downfall of Colonial Life Insurance Company (CLICO), once the largest insurance and financial services company in the Caribbean, provides yet another example of disastrous outcomes resulting from failures in feedback loops and control systems. After being in existence for over seventy years, in 2009, the government of Trinidad and Tobago had to intervene, and governments across the Caribbean had to seek redress for their citizens through the sale of the company's assets, as CLICO was unable to meet its financial obligations to policyholders. Notwithstanding, this was not enough, and it was certainly too late to protect losses from individual policy holders. While the story behind CLICO's collapse is complex, it is clear that its failures were a result of weak internal controls and inadequate regulatory feedback loops, as Caribbean regulators provided insufficient supervision and ineffective intervention despite obvious signs of increasing systemic risk. This lack of prompt regulatory feedback allowed dangerous practices, such as excessive risk-taking and liquidity mismanagement, by the company's leadership to persist unchecked.

> **An Interesting Aside**
>
> An eerie behaviour pattern that is related to a system's elements and its dynamic behaviour is called "entanglement". Although Albert Einstein observed this, it was not until recently, in 2022, that the Nobel Prize for Physics was awarded to three scientists, Alain Aspect, John F. Clauser, and Anton Zeilinger, for their pioneering work in this area. Entanglement, which can be explained through the principles of quantum mechanics, describes a condition where the spin of one atomic particle becomes so interconnected with another, that the state of one atom instantly influences the state of another, regardless of the distance separating them. Since all elements of a system are made up of atoms, it is possible to, therefore, envisage a relationship, a continuum, or connectedness not just between processes within a system, but processes between systems within systems, no matter how far apart they are, irrespective of whether we have the capacity to measure the distance between them. This scientific evidence, unlike any other, provides confirmation to the naysayers who continue to believe that one's actions and beliefs can be totally

isolated, and not have an impact on others who are not just within the same sub-system that they are a part of, but within the overall ultimate system, the universe.

Let's review this chapter. Although the term "system" is used in a prolific manner, across all disciplines, you should now be able to discern if you are dealing with a system if you identify at least the following four properties: elements or parts, a structure or interactions, a purpose, and boundaries. If you do have a system, then you should now be able to appreciate its dynamic behaviour, governed by its multi-dimensional interactions called feedback loops.

Now that you know how to identify whether you are in a system or you are dealing with a system, the next step is identifying what that system is. In the next chapter, I will share some thoughts on how to apply an understanding of particular features that are present in all systems, whether they are natural or man-made, to help you identify the systems you are a part of. Then we will go on to discuss how to use some basic systems principles to understand the interactions within and between systems and other systems.

CHAPTER 3

Identifying the System(s) You Are a Part Of

There are no separate systems. The world is a continuum. Where to draw a boundary around a system depends on the purpose of the discussion.
—**Donella H. Meadows**

The universe is arguably the ultimate and largest whole system we are aware of. Scientific methods can only estimate the size of the observable universe based on speed of light calculations; however, humankind is incapable of determining whether it extends beyond this, and it is quite possible it does, expanding to *infinitum*. Though we are limited by our current capabilities, I believe it would be impossible to establish a conceptual boundary around the whole system of the universe. This is because if we apply the laws of thermodynamics, which govern how energy and matter interact, it is reasonable to assume that the universe is constantly expanding, trending always towards increasing entropy—increasing chaos. Astrophysicists and astro-chemists are currently spending a lot of time and effort on research that would help us gain a deeper understanding of this massive complex system we call our universe.

The work being done in this area is phenomenal, and while an understanding of the universe and other such complex systems is necessary because all systems are connected, this is not the focus of this chapter nor of this book. Instead, we will focus on much smaller, manageable systems within our universe—the types of systems you are more likely to be directly involved with during your time on Earth: the types of systems you want to create, and the ones that are more likely to be within your control.

To achieve the level of sustainability that we all aim for, it is necessary to gain an understanding of what system and systems we are a part of. To do so, a proven successful approach is to first break the larger system into smaller parts, that is, smaller systems. A smaller system is conceptually easier to manage. With a smaller system, we need less information to describe what is happening inside it, and the pathways for information flow, through interactions such as feedback loops, are much shorter. This minimises the delay in receiving information that would influence the system's behaviour. Reducing a large system into smaller manageable systems would, therefore, enhance the efficiency with which we can control and direct that system and improve the effectiveness with which we do so.

The smallest living systems have the capacity to receive information within the shortest time period. With this ability, the system is able to respond quickly to information received through feedback loops, adapting itself in a speedy manner, to any changes in its environment. This ability is intrinsically linked to sustainability, and micro-organisms are far superior in demonstrating this, compared to their larger multi-cellular counterparts, such as the human body.

Boundaries

But how are smaller systems within systems created? As presented in the previous chapter, one of the four basic components of a system is its boundary. A system is created only when its boundaries can be defined. Research conducted in natural science fields such as physics and chemistry has already confirmed that everything is connected within the universe. Based on these scientific theories, principles, and rules, we know that we, and the things we create, are all connected within our universe system, transferring information between the elements within the huge ultimate system via packets of energy. The only way to create a smaller system that is easier for us to manage on our own, and collectively as a team, would be to create a boundary around the system that we want to have control over.

It is important to remember, however, that a system's boundary is not a physical phenomenon. Instead, a system's boundary is conceptual in nature, and this boundary can only be created around a common purpose. The system's boundary will distinguish that system from other systems by its purpose. There may be similarities between the purposes of two different systems, and this often arises when systems have similar structures. However, while there may be similarities in some attributes of systems with similar structures, no two systems are the same, unless their purpose is the same. The ability to identify similar systems is a key asset to improving your system's functions, as it facilitates the use of benchmarking as a tool to track the improvement of your system's performance. This tool must, however, be used with utmost care, because if used wrongly, it could lead to the destruction of your system.

The system's boundaries help to provide you and others within the system with the clarity needed to determine what processes are within your control and what processes are not within your control. Understanding the nature of your system's boundaries, therefore, helps you to manage your system, whether the system is a personal one, your household, or any other organisational system you are associated with. For instance, on the personal level, establishing a clear periphery for your personal system helps you to differentiate your emotions and actions from those of others. Your boundaries, therefore, provide you with clarity on what emotions and actions you need to take responsibility for, which are certainly not those of others. If your boundaries are blurred for your personal systems, as an individual, you may end up consuming your time by taking responsibility for the emotions and actions of others who really do not belong to your personal system.

Notwithstanding, the boundaries of a system can never be completely impervious. Rather, all systems' boundaries are porous, allowing the transfer of information across them. Some boundaries may be more porous than others, but it is impossible to create a boundary that would entirely eliminate the transfer of all energy between them. Even in scientific research, when conducting experiments, it is almost impossible to create perfectly impervious barriers, particularly for the social sciences. For natural sciences such as chemistry, scientists go to great lengths, using expensive and elaborate inert containment measures to achieve isolated spaces to conduct their experiments—and even then, total isolation may be impossible to achieve.

For human systems, however, there are definitely no impervious boundaries. Therefore, you must understand the nature and porosity of your system's boundaries because only with this understanding, can you know how your system interacts with other systems. The interactions between systems will be discussed further in the next chapter, but before we move deeper into this, now that you know a system must have a boundary, you need to know how to conceptualise and create boundaries around the system you are in and the systems you want to create.

Identifying the Real System

You may be reading this book because, no doubt, the term "system" is familiar to you—perhaps you have heard it several times in various spheres of your life. You may, therefore, agree that this term, "system", and its derivatives, such as "systemise" and "systemic", are ubiquitous and are used in almost all disciplines and circumstances, often very loosely—whether or not a true system even exists. But how can we identify when a real system does exist?

We discussed earlier that a system is identified by its purpose. Results from scientific research have confirmed that a system can only exist if there is a common purpose driving its behaviour. It is, therefore, logical that in order to know what system you are a part of and whether you actually are in or interacting with a real system, the first thing to do is to try to determine whether there is a common purpose; and if you believe there is, and you are in that system, it is your job to determine what that purpose is.

To do so, it helps to become mentally still and to be fully present in your environment to feel the beat or energy of the system or systems that you are interacting with. Though it is important to have gleaned background information from reliable sources beforehand, be careful. Too much background information, especially when you are not sure about the reliability of the sources of that information, can create qualia, or a biased frame of reference for your mind that may interfere with your ability to assess and analyse the behaviour patterns around you in an unbiased manner.

For this reason, whenever I am immersed in a new environment, I prefer to enter with just enough background information to be able to avoid any major personal risks. I like approaching my interactions with elements within any new system with a childlike curiosity and innocence. That system may exist within a social setting or workplace environment. Whatever the environment of the system, it is important to try to be present, as much as possible, with an "open mind" and no preconceptions. This state of being may sometimes be misconstrued as naivety, but do not let this common misconception discourage you.

It is necessary to give yourself the opportunity to feel the natural flow of energy within the system, avoiding any preconceived notions and background clutter. Only after you have felt the natural beat of the system are you in a position to thoroughly review all background information in order to support your analysis of what you have observed and to determine the purpose of the system. With your best efforts at obtaining unbiased observations of what is happening to and around you, using all your senses, the behaviour of the system will become clearer to you, and you will get a sense of the system's organic purpose.

For instance, the behaviour of an organisational system may sometimes be described by its organisational culture. This usually refers to the collective patterns of beliefs and values from the personal systems within the organisation and how those collective patterns influence the organisation's daily activities and behaviour. If you are part of an organisational system, it is useful to periodically mentally step away from it and do your best to step away from your personal system as well, in an attempt to establish a "blank page" view of the system. From this stance, you will be better able to observe and determine the behaviour patterns of your organisational system. Assistance can also be sought from appropriate consultants external to your organizational system to help you conduct this exercise in a more objective manner.

Purpose and Intention in Systems

You may find yourself in a system that already has a purpose that is coded and expressed, and the behaviour patterns that you observe and feel align with your understanding of the system's coded declaration of its purpose. It is always great being part of systems like these, especially when the purpose is aligned to that of your personal value system. However, there are times when you may observe actions and behaviour patterns that are not aligned with the system's declared purpose. For instance, you may join an organisation within the health sector, with a declared purpose to save lives. However, you find that there is a lack of risk-based thinking, and it affects the organisation's decision-making processes when it comes to its procurement processes. This consistently results in a compromised quality of the output from the organisation's core processes, resulting in risking lives, instead of saving them. In such instances, the actions and behaviour patterns you observe may be more aligned with the goals of the personal intentions of the humans within the system, which perhaps is to make as much money as possible, and their intentions are not aligned with the declared purpose of the system, i.e., to save lives. At this point, the system is or becomes not the system you thought you were becoming a part of. To appreciate this, let us go deeper into the difference between purpose and intention.

"Purpose" refers to the fundamental reason for the system's existence. A purpose is enduring and deep-rooted, providing a sense of direction for the system. For instance, in the business context, the purpose of an organisation's overall business system ought to be related to the key problem that the business seeks to solve within the market while the purpose of its finance sub-system would be to ensure the profitability or financial health of the business. For example, the declared purpose of a health food company could be: "To nourish lives with wholesome, sustainable foods that contribute to better health and vitality". The organisation's sub-systems could also have their purposes too, but the purposes of these sub-systems should all be aligned with the overall common purpose of the business.

Likewise, within a non-professional context, the purpose of your household system may be to provide a healthy, supportive environment to the members of your household, so that each household member can flourish. Every single system that you are a part of within your lifetime will have a purpose, irrespective of whether that purpose is clarified and declared formally in a coded manner.

"Intention", on the other hand, relates to more immediate cognitive processes in the human's personal system, leading to specific actions to achieve a specific goal. Intention involves making a decision to engage in a certain action or behaviour pattern and planning to execute that decision. Intention is only associated with the human elements within the system, and it is often linked to achieving more immediate, short-term goals. It is invoked by human beings, using the prefrontal cortex of the brain—that is, the part of the brain associated with planning and decision-making. Intention is highly influenced by the transfer of energy or information through feedback loops.

When actions and behaviours result from intentions that are mis- or mal-aligned with the system's declared purpose, the system's structure becomes at risk of changing. When the structure of a system changes drastically, it becomes almost impossible to fulfil its original purpose, if other counteracting measures are not taken. If no action is taken, eventually the system will flourish as a different system, being true to a new, and perhaps, unintended purpose. When this happens, the system you thought you were a part of is no longer the same system.

Note that one intentioned goal can serve different purposes or different systems. Therefore, you need to be careful not to be mistaken, as you may discover a goal that is common to multiple systems, and this goal can confuse you into thinking you are part of a system you did not want to be part of in the first place. Be mindful that where a common goal exists in multiple systems, information will be transferred through these goals, between the different systems sharing common goals. The interactions through which information is transferred will contribute to the structure of the broader system which the multiple similar smaller systems are a part of. To illustrate this, I will use a familiar example of two different systems operating within the same space and time dimensions: a political system and a governance system within a parliamentary system of democracy.

The existence of a strong political party system is the hallmark of a parliamentary governance system, and the head of government, such as a prime minister, is also the leader of the majority party (which is a political system). The prime minister is the human element which is common to both systems. It is, therefore, easy to envisage how an intention to achieve a goal that serves both the purpose of the party system and that of the governance system can exist. The purpose of each system is different. In a democratic system, the purpose of a political party is to gain the majority of votes within the country, in order to achieve or maintain the power to govern that country. The purpose of the governance system, however, is to ensure the well-being of the country's citizens through the provision of adequate public services such as education, healthcare, security, food, and shelter. If you are involved in the processes to achieve a particular goal common to both systems, you need to be part of at least one of the two systems, but not necessarily both. The system that you are a part of will be defined by the boundaries that are conceptualised and created for the purpose of the system, and you ought to always be aware of and know those boundaries.

Another perspective to be aware of is that although a system can be described only by one purpose, it almost always has multiple goals. If you think you have identified multiple purposes, you are either dealing with multiple systems, or you are mistaking the goals for purpose, and you are in one system with multiple goals. For instance, a business organisation could have an established goal to digitise its human resource processes within three years, as well as a goal of upskilling its staff. Both goals would serve the single purpose of one management system, the human resource management system within the business system, and this purpose should be aligned to the overall purpose of the business system.

However, as a human element in one of the sub-systems, you may be tempted to or mistakenly believe that the goal you are helping to achieve is actually the purpose of the business system. This type of confusion could be disastrous to the business system and often occurs when there is poor interaction between the smaller sub-systems within the overall business system. Once this is observed, this could be a sign of a poor structure within the business system.

When you are able to step away and observe at a distance, viewing the system from a higher altitude, it will become possible to discover multiple purposes or multiple systems within the bigger system that you may be part of. This high-level view is necessary for the sustainability of your system, as it helps you to break up your system into smaller, more manageable interconnected parts or sub-systems. This would allow you to gain a better understanding of the interactions or structure within your broader system.

Breaking down bigger systems into smaller systems, which interact well with each other and whose purposes are all aligned, is always much easier to be a part of and to manage. Less information is needed to describe the behaviour of the smaller sub-system, and the delay in receiving information flowing through feedback loops is reduced. This, therefore, gives the smaller systems an opportunity to respond or adapt quickly to whatever changes are taking place around them.

Time for a word of caution: if you identify multiple purposes that are not aligned with each other, you may be interacting with completely different systems, which have totally different structures. Systems like these compete against each other through their interactions. If no control measures are applied, the resources of one system will be depleted by the other system, and the system with the weaker structure will fail or die. This will threaten the sustainability of the overall bigger system that these smaller systems are a part of.

There are several examples of these types of competing interactions among different smaller sub-systems that are a part of a bigger system. The most common ones are the type of economic human systems that interact closely with other systems in nature, such as animal systems, competing, often detrimentally, against these systems. Some of these human systems may be governed by rules such as policies that serve as reinforcing feedback loops to increase a particular stock, say lobster meat, that is shared by both systems, but the purposes of the two systems, the human system and animal system, are different. In this scenario, the human system and the animal system share a common goal: acquiring more lobsters. The system that responds faster to a feedback loop, such as the human system's demand for more lobster meat based on human consumption, will deplete the stock at a faster rate than the reproductive system in the animal kingdom can replenish its stock. If there is no control, both the animal system will die, and the competing human system will also eventually be eliminated.

Let us now review the chapter's key findings. At this point, hopefully, you recognise the need to identify the system you are a part of and understand how to do so, first by determining the system's purpose as well as identifying its boundaries. But this is just the first step to building resilience. Once you identify which system you are in or dealing with, you need to understand how that system interacts with other systems it is surrounded by, since these interactions could either threaten the existence of your system or offer you opportunities to strengthen and grow your system in a sustainable manner.

Earlier, we established that one of the key features of systems are their porous boundaries, through which energy flows in a bidirectional manner—inwards and outwards, from one system to other systems, and vice-versa. This flow of energy has tremendous influence on your system and has the potential to even threaten its existence. Therefore, in the next chapter, we will spend some time discussing some measures to use to help you better understand the relationships between your system and other systems.

CHAPTER 4

Understanding Relationships Within and Between Your System and Other Systems

The most important thing about a system is how it relates to other systems, not how it relates to itself.
—**Russell Ackoff**

We have established that the universe is made up of several different systems and multiple systems within systems. We also know that the behaviour of a system is shaped by the information its processes receive. Since all systems within the universe are connected, it is reasonable to assume that the extent to which your smaller system is sustainable is, in large part, influenced by the activities taking place around it, that is, its external environment. Your system will always respond to its external environment. The length of time it takes to respond and how it responds depends on two key factors: (1) the nature of the systems that your system is surrounded by and (2) the architecture of your system's internal structure and its borders.

Let us now examine the impact of the nature of the relationship between a system and its external environmental system, the relationship between sub-systems within a bigger single system, and how these relationships can affect the performance of the organisational system, as measured by its ability to fulfil its purpose.

External Environment and the Quality Infrastructure

The external environment within which your system operates greatly influences the type of internal structures you need to establish within your system to make your system sustainable. To fully understand this, in this section we will focus on one key aspect of the external environment: quality of infrastructure. You will learn how a good quality infrastructure can benefit and support your own system and how a weak quality infrastructure can threaten the sustainability of your system. In the case of the latter, you will also learn how to respond to build resilience in your system even in the face of an external environment with a weak quality infrastructure.

A society provides value to its citizens through the services and goods produced. These services and goods range from basic healthcare, education, and security services to construction services and more elaborate entertainment and other pleasure-seeking and fulfilling services. These goods and services are produced by various organisational systems operating within a society, and the level of development of the society in which the system operates is measured by the maturity of the society's quality infrastructure.

"Quality infrastructure" is the term used to describe both the soft and hard infrastructure that makes up a society to allow for independent verification and assurance of the quality of services and goods produced within that society. A society's "soft infrastructure" refers to intangible matter, such as processes related to society's governance and management systems, and information technology, while its "hard infrastructure" refers to the brick-and-mortar structures, such as buildings, roads, and equipment.

All societies are, or ought to be, designed with structures to provide their citizens, residents, and visitors with the assurance that they are receiving goods and services of the quality they expect to receive to support the sustainability of their personal system. This assurance in the quality of services and goods offered by and within a country is obtained when the country can demonstrate that it has systems that have at least four purposes. These are:

1. To independently verify measurements used within industry's processes to produce goods and services, as well as measurements used for trading; that is, the exchange of value for money. This is done through the provision of scientific, legal and industrial metrology-related services.
2. To independently attest to the level of competence of individuals and institutions providing key services. This is done through the provision of appropriate accreditation services.
3. To independently certify that the organisations that produce value have processes and produce products that meet national, regional, and international standards. This is done through the provision of process and product certification and other conformity assessment services.

4. To effectively influence the development of national, regional, and globally recognised organisational standards, which are used for, among other things, the quality infrastructure services highlighted above: metrology, accreditation, and conformity assessment services. This is usually demonstrated by the level of participation in standards development processes.

Without the capacity to provide these four pillars of services, it does not matter how strong the country's legislative and judicial capacity is, nor does it matter how much money the country is able to attract through investments, grants, loans, or short-term ventures. All these financial gains and legislative robustness will be useless, unless the governing body of the country is able to build trust among its people and other consumers of the goods and services it produces. No other way has been shown to facilitate the building of trust within a society, unless it is through these assurance mechanisms embedded within the country's quality infrastructure.

Moreover, there is evidence to support a strong correlation between a country's quality infrastructure and the level of corruption in that country. Reports on research conducted in this area have been published by international organizations such as the Organization of Economic Co-operation and Development (OECD), the World Bank and the United Nations Industrial Development Organization (UNIDO). The evidence strongly suggests that the appropriateness and maturity of the country's quality infrastructure is inversely proportional to the level of corruption that exists and is tolerated in the country.

An understanding of the external environment in which your system is operating, such as the maturity level of the quality infrastructure of the country, is important for many reasons, but here, I will focus on just one. If your organisational system is operating within an external environment that has weak quality infrastructural systems, the amount of money you will need to invest into your system to provide assurance to the people your system serves, and consequently to build resilience in your system, would be astronomical. Therefore, unless you have access to unlimited financial resources that you have no accountability for, with this financial burden, your organisation will be at a much higher risk of failure compared to a system operating within an environment that is characterised by a strong, mature quality infrastructure.

The internal structure of an organisational system must be engineered in a manner to suit its environment or society. If a society that the system is operating in is characterised by a culture that has been nurtured within an environment with a weak quality infrastructure or one that is not fully matured, then the internal structure of the organisational system will need to be designed with an internal structure characterised by a strong compliance sub-system to minimise the occurrence and perception of corruption compared to an organisation operating within a society with a strong, mature quality infrastructure.

The External Environment's Influence on Your System

Once you understand the maturity level of the external environment that your system is operating in, you can design and build an appropriate internal structure for your system to thrive in that environment. The structure must be such that it compensates for the weaknesses of the external environment and allows you to have a level of control over the direction of the processes within your system. The porosity of your system's boundaries would depend on how much and what information you would like to flow from the external environment into your system to influence your internal processes. Likewise, the strength of your system's own internal control mechanisms would depend on the level of stability you need for your internal processes and the pace at which you would like your overall system to change to suit the changing external environment.

As counterintuitive as it may seem, just as it is with fast cars and their robust braking systems, the faster the pace of change you desire for your system, the more robust the controls you need at the process levels within your system. These controls are usually in the form of rules, such as policies, procedures, laws, and incentives. However, never make the cardinal error of importing control mechanisms from other systems into your system, no matter how similar the purpose of that system may appear to be to yours. The purposes of no two systems are identical, as the elements within different systems are never all identical. For instance, even if two systems may have identical non-human elements, the human elements within the two different systems are usually not the same.

Again, for re-emphasis, I will repeat this here: the way in which the brain interprets information is influenced by qualia and driven by emotion. This, in turn, influences intentions, which impact the goals that humans focus on achieving. Consequently, while another system may have a purpose similar to yours, both systems will not have the same goals. Goals, like purpose, influence the behaviour of the system. Therefore, the only value, which is an important value, of the experiences of other systems to you, is your ability to benefit from the lessons learnt by the other systems. In other words, it can be beneficial to note which control mechanisms were a success or failure to them. Considering the experiences of other systems is not the same as copying them. Never copy. Considering the experiences of other systems should assist you to adapt and innovate your own processes to suit the peculiar needs of your system in order to ensure that your control mechanisms are "fit for purpose".

The Internal Environment: Culture of Quality

Thus far in this chapter, we have examined the relationship between your system and other systems external to it. At this point, we will shift to looking at the internal structure of your system. We will examine the attributes of internal environments that have been proven to demonstrate support for the sustainability of systems irrespective of the external environment of the system. These attributes, altogether, are frequently referred to as a "culture of quality".

The principles of a "culture of quality" have been aptly espoused by the International Organization for Standardization (ISO) and are captured in the ethos of their management systems' standards. These management systems' standards provide non-propriety guidance for high performance in various areas, such as quality, risk, environment, food safety, personal security, and information security. Based on international best practice and standards, an organisational system is characterised as having a good culture of quality when the following characteristics are demonstrated:

    1. **Leadership Commitment:** Leaders at all levels within the organisation demonstrate a strong commitment to having the products and services produced meet quality

standards, and the organisation's strategy and resources are prioritised to allow for this.

2. **Employee Engagement:** Employees are empowered and encouraged to take responsibility for the quality of their work, and there is an emphasis on training and development of the human elements within the system. This ensures that all team members have the necessary skillsets to achieve the goals set by the organisation in an efficient and effective manner.

3. **Customer Focus:** Organisations with a strong culture of quality actively listen to both their internal and external customers, ensuring that information is received from customers through various feedback mechanisms. Importantly, these organisations use this information to drive improvements within the processes within their organisational system and to foster customer loyalty.

4. **Transparency and Communication:** There is transparency with the system's processes and effective communication with all stakeholders, which includes employees and suppliers alike. When all stakeholders are "in the know" with respect to the information they need, this helps to support alignment of the system's intentions and goals with the purpose of the system.

5. **Collaboration and Teamwork:** This is a key feature of all successful and sustainable organisations. Collaboration is needed across all components, sub-systems, or departments within the organisational system to ensure, among other things, that decisions taken are based on the receival of adequate information. Note that while

humans can collaborate between systems, each with its own purpose, teamwork can only exist at the level where the humans share one common purpose. This will be addressed in greater depth in a later chapter.

6. **Continual Improvement:** The internal and external recipients of the services and products produced by organisations are all human, and we know that the qualia and needs of human beings are constantly changing. The organisation, therefore, must regularly evaluate its processes and sub-systems to identify areas for improvement and to implement changes based on the changes in the needs and expectations of the humans they serve. This is necessary to enhance the quality of the products and services produced.

When all the sub-systems within your organisation, which includes its governance systems such as compliance systems, and its operational improvement systems such as quality management systems, demonstrate these six attributes associated with a strong culture of quality, your sub-systems will be better able to operate in an integrated manner, minimising any unintended 'silo effects'. This means that all your sub-systems within your organisational system will be networking with each other effectively to achieve the purpose that the system was created for. As stated at the beginning of this book, there is no other alternative if you want your system to survive and achieve resilience in this era of "Industry 5.0".

The Impact of Corrupting Relationships

Obviously detrimental to a system is one whose internal environment has been corrupted. Here, we will examine how corruption works to weaken and destroy a system and how to set up structures within your system to avoid the possibility of corruption from occurring.

It is well understood that corruption, by virtue of its definition, stymies the growth and development of any system. The Organisation for Economic Co-operation and Development (OECD) defines corruption as "the abuse of entrusted power for private gain". This private gain could be financial or non-financial. Corruption can include embezzlement and other acts of fraud, or just simply manipulation of the decision-making powers that the office holds, to benefit the holder of the office. Surely, as we established earlier, the purpose of an organisational system can never be to enrich only one person, even when that one person is the one who has established that organisational system. The purpose of an organisational system must always be to solve a problem in nature, society, or the ultimate universal system it is a part of. Therefore, if corruption is rampant within an organisational system, resources will tend to be diverted from being used for activities focused on achieving the organisation's intended purpose and, instead, used for fulfilling the purpose of an individual's personal system. In so doing, this diversion of needed financial and other resources inevitably affects the quality of services and products produced by the organisation because very often, the quality of the necessary inputs into the system's processes are reduced or compromised. This leads to inefficiencies and ineffectiveness of the system's processes, resulting in reputational and financial losses - both of which are major strategic risks for organisations.

Moreover, when corruption is rampant within an organisational system, the architecture of the system's structure and interactions become compromised, as trust within the system becomes eroded.

Since organisational systems are human systems, trust is essential for effective communication, collaboration, and engagement between the human elements within the organisation. In the absence of trust, you can, therefore, expect that the quality of information received and perceived by human beings within the organisation through the system's feedback process loops will be poor.

In such an environment, your system's processes will likely be responding to false information or no information from key feedback loops, as the humans within the system will not care to share information. As seen in the previous chapter, a system by its very nature is dynamic. It will, therefore, respond to any information received, whatever the quality. This is because the primitive part of the organ used to interpret information in the personal system, the human brain, does not know how to decipher between false or true information, nor between good or bad quality information. This has been proven by neuroscience, which demonstrates that the brain responds to any stimulus. Knowing this, it makes sense to invest in mechanisms for cleaning the data or other information that your system receives. These mechanisms ought to be embedded into the structure of your system to ensure that both human and non-human operators within your system always receive high-quality information for processing. A key takeaway is that, as much as possible, you need to minimise the risk of your system's processes responding to the wrong information. Therefore, careful thought is required regarding the structure of your system.

In addition, you need to ensure that your structure allows for your processes to receive a balance of information in a bi-directional manner. If it is designed in a manner to only receive information from one direction, this could affect the stability of its processes by forcing them to be pushed more in one direction and not achieve equilibrium within the system. If you are implementing transformational change initiatives, then this may not be a problem for the short term, as you would know the direction of the quantum leap you want your processes to take.

Rules are an important tool for controlling the flow of information in the direction that you want within your processes and minimising the risk of corruption. So important is it that a separate chapter, Chapter 6, is dedicated to explaining the role and function of rules to improve a system's performance. However, at this juncture, it is important to know that the effective implementation of appropriate rules, such as policies and procedures, is a non-negotiable requirement in order to prevent acts of corruption. Not only do rules define and maintain the structures within organisational systems, but in the absence of formal rules, there can be no clarity on what constitutes dishonest activities within your system. Dishonesty is considered a form of corruption. But how can you determine if the human in the system is behaving dishonestly if your system has weak or no rules at all? The behaviour of someone holding an office of power can only be deemed to be dishonest if the system that person is in has the appropriate rules made known to them and only then, if these rules are implemented effectively.

In the absence of rules, corruption within the system can only be determined relative to best practices and internationally recognised standards belonging to external systems. In these instances, at best, the determination of corruption will be based on the subjectively perceived unethical behaviour of the individual. This becomes very fuzzy, and it would be problematic for ensuring accountability within the system.

Let's review this chapter. Having read this chapter, you should now have a better understanding of how the interactions or relationships within the internal environment of your system, and its interaction with its external environment, can influence the viability of your system. In addition, it is my hope that you can appreciate the importance of understanding the external environment within which your system operates and how this understanding can influence you on the type of internal structures you need to establish within your own system. Indeed, we saw how the level of the maturity of the society within which your system operates, as measured by the maturity of its quality infrastructure, could have a huge impact on your operational costs.

Understanding the internal and external context of your system is critical for developing an appropriate strategy for growing and building resilience into your system. To do so effectively, it is always useful to seek the assistance of a human, with personal systems that are external and independent of your organisational system, such as an external consultant. Securing the assistance of an external consultant to conduct an analysis of the internal and external context of your organisation minimises the negative impact of biases in the interpretation of the data obtained and helps with a more effective diagnosis on the issues to be addressed and gaps to be closed to achieve your strategic, tactical, and operational objectives. Feel free to contact us at KMA Consulting—www.kma.consulting - if you need help in this area.

Now that you are armed with the knowledge of systems from Part 1, we transition to Part 2 of this book. In this second part, you will go on to learn how to create the type of system that you want and the type that you will feel in harmony with.

PART II

DESIGNING THE SYSTEM YOU WANT TO BE A PART OF

CHAPTER 5

Discovering the Processes That Exist Within Your System

If you can't describe what you are doing as a process, you don't know what you're doing.
—**Sir W.E. Deming**

In this section of the book, we will delve a bit deeper into understanding the anatomy and mechanics of a system. Yes, as "non-sexy" as this may be considered, an understanding of this is necessary if you are to develop the skillset related to systems thinking, that is needed for the survival of your system in this era. For instance, as you will see later on in this chapter, understanding the processes that exist in your system will give you the information needed to design and establish structures or interactions, such as feedback loops, that are necessary to build resilience into your system.

You may have found yourself within an organisational system, which was formed organically because of the growing demand for a product you or someone else developed. This often happens with entrepreneurs who start off by trial and error and suddenly find themselves having to add more and more resources to produce more and more product.

To clarify, a "product", in the context of this book, refers to either a tangible item, such as a food product, a car, a painting, or a bag; or, it could be an intangible product, such as an IT software programme, legal services, health services, parenting, companionship, or homemaking. Simply put, a product is the result of the value created by processes within a system, and that product is used as input into another process.

This other process could be within the same system, or it could belong to an entirely different system. The means through which it is transferred as an output from one process to become an input into another process may not require any human interaction. For instance, in a mechanical system, you may have an output of an IT process, such as the result of an analysis of primary data points obtained from monitoring a particular attribute. This is usually referred to as "metadata". This metadata could be used as a direct input into another IT process, which triggers a particular chain of activities or responses by an engine.

Although mechanical systems are usually always part of the sub-systems of organisational systems, there will also be sub-systems within the organisation, where a human being is used as a vehicle through which the transfer of the product or output from one process to another process takes place. For example, the result of the analysis of the data obtained may have to be evaluated by a human before a decision is taken to use it as an input into another process. There are several other examples that can be used to demonstrate the intervention of a human being in the transfer of an output from one process in the organisational system to be used as an input into another process. This output could range from a letter produced by administrative processes or a report produced by a compliance or audit process, to a component of a final product. For now, it is important to know that when the transfer of the product takes place through a human being, in management systems sciences, this human is referred to as the "recipient" of the product, whether it is tangible, such as goods, or intangible, such as services.

The value of the product produced by the system's processes is created by using resources. These resources could be any input into the process, such as energy, documentation, money, or thoughts or actions resulting from critical thinking of the human mind. In systems' lingo, the product produced is often referred to as the "stock" of the system, and its "level", or value, serves as key information to which the system's processes respond.

The system receives information related to its stock level and value through feedback loops. This means that information related to the stock of the system plays a key role in influencing how the system behaves or responds. As we saw in Chapter 1, where we discussed the role of feedback loops, some of the system's feedback loops may serve as reinforcing feedback loops, causing the system's processes to produce more of the same product or stock. Alternatively, some feedback loops may serve as negative feedback loops, or balancing feedback loops, causing the system's processes to respond in an opposite direction, resulting in a reduction of its stock's value or levels.

In fields related to social sciences, reinforcing feedback loops may create what is known as "vicious cycles", when they are reinforcing the system's response towards a negative outcome. For example, in an economics context, a decrease in consumer spending can lead to lower business profits, which may, in turn, lead to lay-offs, which further reduces consumer spending, perpetuating the cycle.

Alternatively, some feedback loops could lead to "virtuous cycles", promoting positive development of the system. For example, in a business system, investing money in training employees can lead to higher productivity, which, in turn, leads to greater profits for the business. The business can then invest more in employee benefits and training, and this allows for a continuation in the cycle of improvement and growth.

Whether or not the product of the process is transferred via a human intermediary, its value is always determined by the receiver. For instance, in nature, the receiver could be a microorganism, or at the molecular level, a compound. In a business context, the recipient of the product produced by a business's processes is the customer or client, and this product is usually exchanged through trade for money or some other consideration. In a personal system, the product could be a sense of well-being, and the recipient could be a friend, husband, wife, mother, father, daughter, or son.

Feedback loops will be created through the interaction between the recipient of the product and the system's processes through an exchange of energy in the form of information. The quality of the information received through these feedback loops is determined by the strength of the interaction between the receiver and the system, the latter, serving as the giver. The higher the quality of the information received, the better the system is able to respond. For example, if we go back to the example of cooking rice that we used in Chapter 2, the information on the indicator being monitored was the temperature measurements. This information could be considered fit for purpose, meaning high in quality, as it serves as an excellent measurement to determine when the water is boiling and, therefore, when to add the rice. However, in addition to being fit for purpose, the information ought to also be expressed in a clear, unambiguous manner. If there is a time lag between when it is obtained and when the user needs to access it, the information should be stored under conditions that protect its integrity, by mitigating risks of it being corrupted. If it is corrupted, the quality of information would be decreased. This is one of the reasons that organisations spend so much money investing in cyber-security measures, to protect the integrity of their information stored in the cloud, for instance. Note, however, the metrics to determine and measure the quality of information needed ought to be established by the governing body of the organisational system. This will be determined by balancing the needs of all the stakeholders of the organisational system, including the recipients of the organisation's products and services.

Another key aspect of feedback loops and the transfer of information to be considered is speed. The faster the system receives information, the quicker it is able to respond. This is why if you are accountable for the performance of the system's processes, you want to be in a position where you receive high-quality information at a reasonable frequency to put you in a better position to predict the system's behaviour. In an earlier chapter, we saw the disastrous effect of the directors of a company receiving true information on the financial health of the organization, but in a delayed manner. This company, Enron, no longer exists.

Perhaps the organisational system that you are in appears to be doing well from the outside, and sometimes, it feels like it is doing well from the inside too. Overall, the product produced is considered by its recipients to be of good quality, and these recipients are generally happy most of the time. But sometimes, it can feel like chaos exists within your organisation. You may receive a complaint from the recipients about the quality of your product or service. You feel uneasy as a result, especially if the same type of complaint is received more than once. You believe that things could be better. This can be terrifying, as you begin to fear that from the outside, recipients external to your system may begin to perceive that internally your organisational system is not doing well at all. This perception threatens to weaken confidence in the products you produce.

In addition, you may be concerned that there are opportunities you want to take advantage of to expand and grow your organisation, but your organisational system does not have the capacity to do so. You know that if confidence is weakened in the value of your products, then a vicious cycle could easily be created. For instance, in a business setting, as the demand for your product weakens, this will result in less revenue from sales of your service or goods. With less cash coming into the business, you are unable to pay for critical resources and unable to invest in creating new products to sustain the business in a constantly changing environment. Indeed, if nothing is done to reverse this trend, the vicious cycle will continue, and the business system will spiral downwards until it crashes. How do you take control of a situation like this to avert a major disaster?

To control the situation, you must first break the links or connections within the vicious cycle. This means that you must restructure and change the existing points of interactions within your organisational system that allows for energy transfer in the feedback loop that is responsible for reinforcing the negative response, or vicious cycle. To do this, you need to create a new structure that supports the formation of a virtuous cycle. But you cannot do this if you do not know what processes exist within your system. It is, therefore, important that you first identify and understand what processes actually exist within your organisation.

Within any system, there are two types of processes: core processes and supporting processes. A core process is considered to be a series of activities that are linked to each other, in a linear, logical manner, to produce an output that has value to a recipient external to your system. In a business organisational system, this output or product could be the good or service that is traded, such as the meal produced by the restaurant or the packaged juice drink produced by a beverage manufacturing plant. For your personal system, this product could be intangible, such as care or love that is received by the person with whom you have a relationship.

On the other hand, a supporting process is considered to be a series of activities that are linked to each other, in a linear, logical manner, to produce an output that has value to a recipient within your system. This recipient is sometimes referred to as an "internal customer". Supporting processes are vital to the survival or sustenance of your core processes, as they provide resources at various points within the chain of their activities, which could be used as inputs for core processes. These resources are supplied by your supporting processes to your core processes via the interactions between the two sets of processes.

An example of supporting processes within a business organisational system would be administrative processes, finance processes, auditing processes, human resource management processes, governing processes, or any other process that does not produce a product that is traded but produces products that are necessary for the core processes to function. For instance, in a legal firm, such a supporting process would be conflict-of-interest checking processes, and in a food manufacturing plant, it could be sampling and testing processes. Whilst there may be similar types of supporting processes across various organisations, there will always be some supporting processes unique to the sector or industry in which an organisation is operating. Likewise, some of the core processes in organisations operating within the same sector may be similar. However, no two business systems will have the same processes, as these systems are human systems, serving humans. And remember, no two humans have identical personal systems, as each human is shaped by their own experiences, which are unique to each individual.

Know that any system you are in or interacting with has both sets of processes—core and supporting—co-existing with each other, whether or not you choose to identify them. If you are the type to believe that by some stroke of luck and chance, or perhaps through some divine intervention, the processes within your system will change on their own, in the direction you want them to go, then you do not need to read the rest of this book. If, however, you are in a system, whether it is an organisational one or a personal one, that you wish to change, and you believe that you have agency over its processes—that is, you can take control and make some changes—then the rest of this book is for you because as you read further, you will learn how to identify and map out the processes that exist within your system and steer these processes in the direction you want them to go.

Remember, you are part of many systems, and surely, you would not be interested in being responsible for or even being a part of changing all of them. This would be an impossible task to accomplish. However, throughout your life cycle, once you are old enough to reason, there will be, and always has been, a system you can change or have attempted to change. Even if you do nothing deliberate, systems are continuously changing organically, and these changes are influenced by their existing structure. If you want to engineer these changes, however, you must first identify the processes that exist and then determine how these processes interact with each other, the latter being related to understanding the system's structure.

Mapping Your Activities and Processes

A core process can be discovered by first identifying an output that is of value to a recipient, which could be a human or entire organisation, external to your system's boundary. Once you have identified this output, you can now trace the activities or actions within your system that create this value as an end-product. During this discovery phase, your main goal is to understand the flow of information between these activities, which ultimately results in the production of the output or product created. You may wish to jot this down on paper, connecting the activities with lines or arrows, identifying which points within the chain of activities and what resources are required as input to allow for the progression of the activities to produce the end-product. This is called "mapping your processes", and the result, in systems science, is called a flowchart. The first diagram below offers a generic framework for developing your process map while the second diagram offers a more specific example of a simplified process map for book production.

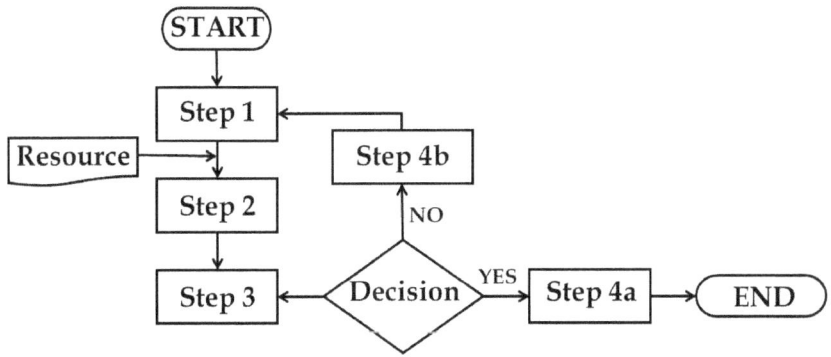

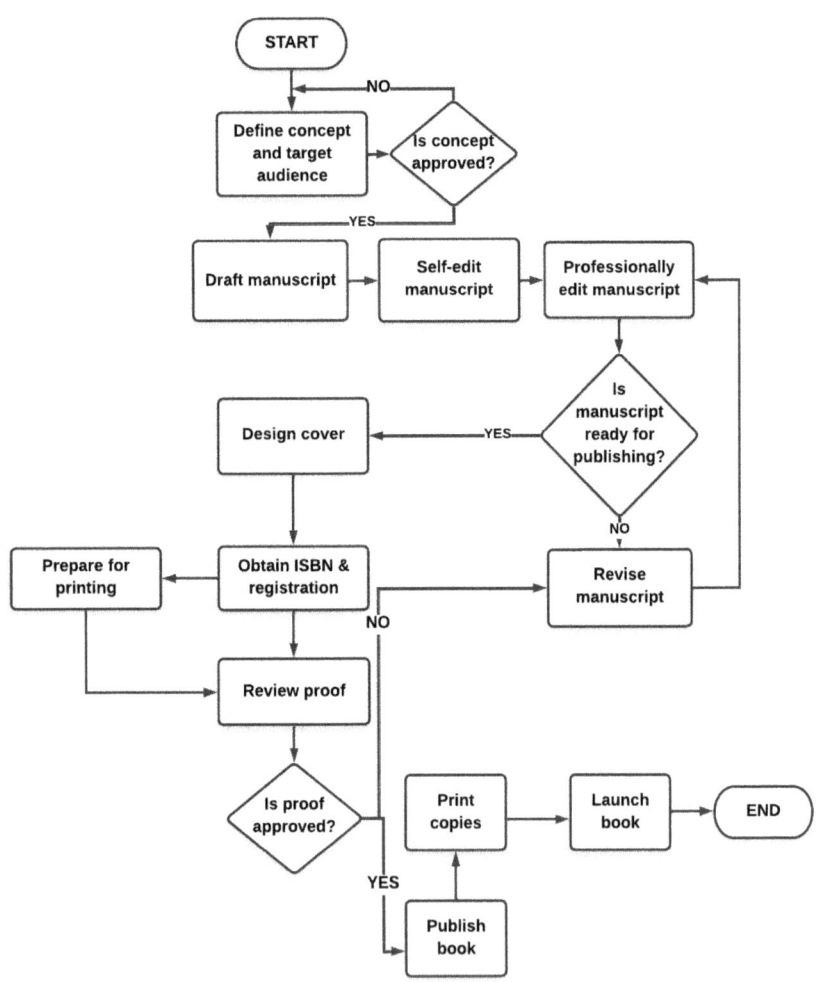

Once you have identified the resources needed for your core processes, you need to discover which processes within your system are responsible for the production of these resources that serve as inputs into your core processes. These processes will be your supporting processes. For instance, for the processes involved in drafting the manuscript in the book production process map reflected above, if you are the author, you may hire someone to do the typing or secretarial services to document your ideas. These processes will be considered supporting processes, as they are needed to support the production of your ideas into the key output, the book, which will be traded.

You need to repeat this investigation to discover all activities in your system that are linked to produce any other outputs that are necessary for your core processes to survive to produce the final end product. For instance, using the same book production process highlighted above, you would need to get the cover of your book designed in order for you to move on to the printing stage. Again, you may outsource this process and hire a design artist to do this. The processes involved in designing your book cover would be another supporting process.

Again, you may wish to jot these other activities down on paper, connecting them with lines or arrows, and identifying the points within the chain of activities and what resources are needed as input to allow for the progression of the activities to produce its end product. Continue this process until you are sure that you have accounted for all activities that relate to the production of the product or service your system produces. For example, for book production, you need a number of inputs to draft your manuscript, such as a clearly defined concept and target audience. You need to identify all the activities to be undertaken to produce those inputs and link these processes to the book production flowchart at the appropriate points.

The level of formality you choose to use to document your processes is entirely up to you, and it would also depend on the size of the system you are dealing with. You saw an example of a simpler process map in the earlier chapter, which demonstrated how to cook rice, while the one about book production shown above reflects a greater complexity. You can also hire a consultant to utilise specialised software programmes to generate your process maps for your organisational system. I highly recommend this activity, and I would be happy to assist you in this area. Once the processes and their interactions within your system are clear to you and other decision-makers within the organisation, strategy formulation for the growth and sustainability of the organisation becomes easier and effective.

If it is your personal system, you may choose to just keep a mental map of these processes. If, however, it is an organisational system, and you want to ensure that all other humans operating within the system have the same understanding of what that process is, you would definitely want to consider mapping your key processes in a simplified manner. You could even seek help in taking it a step further, to map out the interactions between all the processes within your system to create a snapshot, or pictogram, that provides information at a glance, about the connections between all the processes within your system. This process map of your system will demonstrate the structure of your system in a manner that ought to be easily understood by everyone within your organisation.

Similar processes within your organisation can be grouped together to form smaller systems or sub-systems within your main system. You would recall that smaller systems are easier to manage. Earlier in this book, we established that information flows more easily within smaller systems, and overall, smaller systems are less complex. Consequently, less information is needed to describe them. But before you can create smaller sub-systems within your broader organisational system, you first need to be clear on what processes exist before you can group the similar ones together in a logical manner.

The first part of this book expounded upon the importance of understanding the purpose of the system you are in, and this importance cannot be overemphasised. Understanding the purpose of your system is so crucial to its sustainability that all the processes you identify ought to align with your system's purpose. If you discover that the output and your core processes are not aligned with your system's purpose, then in reality, the system you are dealing with is not the one you believed you were in.

If this is what you uncover, you have two options available to you. The first option is to initiate or play an active role in restructuring the system, if you have agency over it. Alternatively, if you do not have any agency over the system's operations, the second option available is to leave the system you have discovered not to be aligned to the purpose you believed were contributing to achieving. In a situation like this, a "do-nothing" approach, whilst remaining in the same system you discovered not to be producing outputs aligned with its purpose, is certainly not an option, or rather, ought not to be even considered, if your personal goal is the prosperity and sustainability of your personal systems. Staying in such a system which is not in harmony with your purpose, goals, and intentions will create unnecessary stress on the most important aspect of your personal system—your health and well-being.

As we proceed with the following chapters, you will learn how to restructure the systems that you choose to invest energy in restructuring in order to create the system that you want. However, before you do so, let us spend some time in the next chapter learning how you can use rules as a critical tool to support the structure you want to create.

CHAPTER 6

Systems' Rules: Policies, Laws, Procedures, Standards, and Assumptions

Language can often be dismissed as being trivial, or the 'soft stuff', whenever attention is given to it during discussions on matters that are not directly related to linguistics. However, as we noted earlier, language is one of the key tools we use to transfer information between humans within a system. Therefore, the way in which the spoken word is interpreted by the receiver is extremely powerful in influencing the behaviour of human elements within a system. Consequently, if we do not get it right from the onset, that is, if no effort is made to ensure that there is a common interpretation and understanding of the words used within a system, there is a huge risk of creating unpredictable outputs from processes within the system. In turn, this could result in disastrous outcomes for anyone who is attempting to direct and control that system.

So crucial is language to the success of a system, I thought it necessary to dedicate a separate chapter in this book to bring clarity to the following terms often associated with governing and managing processes within systems: rules, policies, procedures, standards, penalties, and assumptions. Throughout my years of working with clients and colleagues on initiatives to improve organisational performance, I have found that there continues to be a lack of appreciation and consequently little attention given to establishing common terminology that is used within organisational systems.

Rules

All systems need rules to survive as a system. The connotations associated with rules have really been unfortunate, particularly within the developing world and geographic regions that have a past characterised by slavery and colonisation. This is unfortunate, as it is impossible for a system—both natural and man-made—to exist without rules. The ethos of thinking in systems is about examining, directing, and managing the interrelationships and dependencies among all the parts within the system. A rule can, therefore, be described as a constraint that defines how the components of the system interact with each other to function as a whole. We are all familiar with rules, as they exist in all the systems that we have had to navigate through from our birth to this point, and beyond, within our lifetime. Some of these rules could be informal or formal, explicitly expressed or implied. The figure below gives some examples of the types of rules in systems, that you no doubt would already be familiar with, but perhaps never viewed as rules.

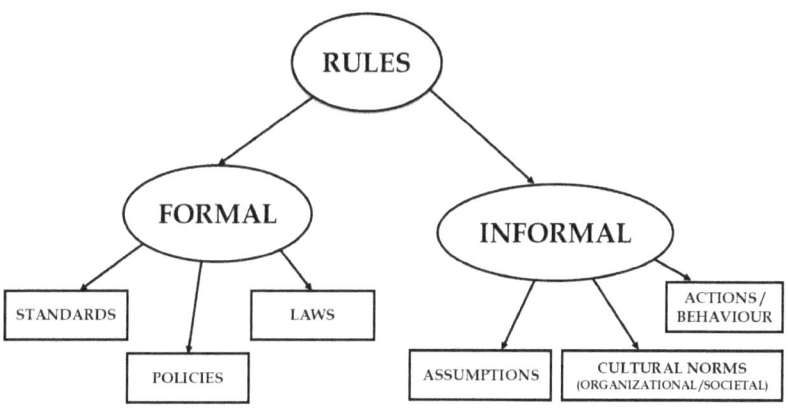

Rules in systems play a powerful role in influencing the mindset of humans in these systems. Rules are established to carry out many functions, such as setting boundaries to control the flow of energy, in whatever form, between various processes and sub-systems within the organisational system or between the whole system and its external environment. These boundaries, whether internal or structural, or peripheral, help to manage the interactions between the components of the system, and they often assist in preventing conflicts and ensuring coherence of behaviour patterns within the system. Rules could also be created to channel information flow in a particular direction to establish feedback loops within the system and to ensure that the correct information is received by the appropriate components within the system in a timely manner. This is crucial to providing a mechanism to adjust the behaviour of the processes within your system.

As we will expand later, the ability to self-adjust is critical for the survival of your system, as this capability allows it to swiftly adapt to internal changes and external pressures. Self-adapting capability also enables the system's processes to quickly regain and maintain equilibrium if it is lost at any point in time.

Rules also provide a means for standardising processes or the behaviour of various components within a system. As we will see in the next chapter, process standardisation is essential to grow and to build resistance into your system, as it helps to reduce variability within the system and its sub-systems. This, in turn, helps to not only improve performance efficiency of your system, but importantly, it helps the human elements within your system with predictability. Later in this book, you will get a better appreciation of the relationship between predictability and the success of your system.

In summary, rules provide a means of control and regulation of the processes within your system. By controlling the flow of information, allocation of resources, and sequence of actions, rules guide your processes to produce the desired outcomes. In essence, they influence the overall dynamics of the system by maintaining its integrity, stability, and efficiency while ensuring that the system achieves its purpose—whatever you wish this to be. There can be no game without rules, and I am sure you appreciate this. Why, then, would we want to eliminate rules from our living systems, which are essentially the game of life?

Policies

So important are rules to the establishment and survival of systems, I think it is necessary to unpack some of these rules that we often encounter in the management of systems. Different rules within systems usually have a complex relationship with each other, but these can be described as hierarchical and supportive. In the last section of this book, we will delve deeper into this relationship, but for now, it would suffice to establish a common understanding between popular terms used in governing and managing systems that are a part of personal and organisational systems. One of the terms which is placed at the top of this hierarchical structure is "policies".

All human systems are guided always by basic values, objectives, and principles for making decisions within the system. These are usually reflected in the policies of the system, which all ought to be aligned with achieving the system's purpose, through its mission. Often, particularly for personal systems and small organizational systems with one or two humans, these principles are not expressed in any formal documentation. But they do exist, nonetheless. If there is no formal documentation expressing the policies guiding a system, you can simply observe how the humans within the system make decisions over a period of time to obtain a good idea of the informal policies that are guiding that system.

Because policies are used to guide decision-making processes within the system, they are usually established by the creators or owners of the system. In organisational systems, this authority, depending on the type of organisation, usually rests with the governing body and member stakeholders or owners. When policies are documented, they are described as being formalised, as they are expressed in language that provides for a means of standardising its interpretation by anyone operating within the system. Formalisation of policies allows for this, even in the absence of the humans who have established the system and developed these policies.

Furthermore, the language used to describe the policy should be very general, and not detailed, to allow for flexibility and discretion in its interpretation for application over time. Notwithstanding, the words used to describe the policy should be clear, as this would provide the framework for developing more detailed specific procedures, standards, and rules, which provide information on the "how" and are used to control the processes within the system.

Moreover, it is crucial that the policy developed is expressed in a manner that can be implemented and enforced, as compliance with policies is critical to setting and maintaining the organisational system's culture and practices. Compliance with policies, therefore, ought to be mandatory for all humans within the system, and enforceable by the governing body of that system.

Procedures

The next level in the hierarchy of system documentation are "procedures". Procedures are usually more detailed than policies, as they provide clear instructions on how to perform specific tasks or activities within a process or a set of similar processes within a system. The procedure would contain work instructions, that is the sequence of steps to be taken within the process. It would also provide clarity on the process requirements and on the tools and materials needed to execute the activities, as well as who is responsible for what within the process. Procedures add meaning to flowcharts and process maps, which were discussed in the previous chapter, as a critical tool used to help you discover the processes within your system.

All policies are implemented through procedures. Therefore, a well-designed and documented procedure would ensure that the system's processes operate in coherence with the system's policies, which, in turn, ought to be aligned to the system's purpose. Well-documented procedures provide clarity to the humans within the system by providing clear guidance on how to perform tasks.

This reduces confusion and the possibility of errors. Additionally, well-developed procedures ought to ensure that the guidance and instructions given are aligned with regulatory compliance and other obligations, including agreed standards. Further, a good procedure always ensures accountability within the human system by defining who is responsible for what. Since systems and their processes are invisible and cannot be touched, a procedure represents the best attempt to document and "feel" the system's processes, providing a common language which facilitates the review of the system's performance for improvement.

Standards

The next hierarchy level of documentation associated with the direction and management of the system's processes are "standards". Good procedures ought to refer to the standards agreed by the leadership of the system that would be used to guide the performance of process activities within the system. Standards ought to be established and referred to in the system's procedures to guide the quality of the output of the system's processes. In the next two chapters, I will discuss in greater detail how standards can be used to stabilise the processes within your system to allow you to make the continual improvements needed to sustain its operation.

However, at this point, it is sufficient to understand that in systems lingo, a standard is considered a rule and ought not to be mistaken as and used interchangeably with the term "law". Too often the two terms are used interchangeably within the organisational context, and this creates confusion. While laws can reference standards, the two have distinct meanings and serve different purposes.

When dealing with human systems, or rather when approaching anything using a system's mindset, a clear understanding of the purpose of the system's activities, processes, and elements is crucial for you to act or behave in a manner that supports the system's survival. We know that words are a tool used by humans to communicate and provide clarity to our interpretation machine, the brain. Therefore, it is totally unacceptable to interchange words with different meanings so loosely within your system.

A standard is a documented agreement that contains criteria or technical specifications that can be used consistently as a guide to achieving the objectives set by the human elements within the system. In relation to organisational systems, standards are used to ensure that the processes within the system and their outputs are fit for the system's purpose and objectives. When standards are used, the aim really is to achieve a common level of performance and to ensure that the output of processes is compatible. Standards provide guidelines and best practices and offer users flexibility to make changes and adapt. Laws are mandatory rules in complex jurisdictional systems and operate within the external environment of your organisational system. Non-compliance with laws attracts penalties or sanctions such as fines and/or imprisonment.

Within an organisational system, some specifications in the standard being used could create a rule which would provide a specific directive mandating a particular action to be taken. The rule created is specific and prescriptive, offering no flexibility on the action to be taken. When a rule is created within a system, failure to comply with that rule ought to result in a penalty, and some form of corrective action should be taken as a result. In Chapter 7, we will discuss how some rules can be used to stabilise processes within your system. However, for now, please understand that once a rule is set, resources must be applied to monitor compliance with this rule, as compliance is mandatory.

Penalties

For your organisational systems, you need to decide what penalties you want to put in place to ensure that your system's processes behave in the way you want it to. There should be a thread of alignment tying all your rules within your system to the purpose of your overall organisational system. Rules that are set to ensure compliance with your processes and their outputs with agreed standards may attract less punitive actions, if broken. In fact, the actions initiated as a consequence of rules broken at that level really ought to be focused on re-calibrating or re-balancing the process back to its stable level. Data received regarding this type of rule breaking ought to be embraced because it gives you information to steer the response of your system's processes back into the direction you want it to go.

However, the rules set to ensure adherence to your system's policies may attract more severe actions or penalties if broken. This is because policies establish the framework for ensuring that the purpose of the system is realised. Once a rule linked to your policies is broken, the action ought to be complete removal of the root cause for breaking of this type of rule, from your system.

We established at the beginning of this book that systems operate within systems, and these interact with other systems. Your organisational system will, therefore, be operating within a broader system. Although you or your governing body sets the rules for your system, it is necessary to know the relevant rules of all the systems that your system is a part of and interacts with. For instance, as indicated earlier, the rules that you set must be aligned and be consistent with the rules of the jurisdictional system you are operating in, which are the laws. If they are not, your system would be operating illegally, and this would pose a strategic risk, as non-compliance with regulatory requirements within the space in which you are operating would threaten the existence of your system.

Assumptions

There are also rules right within your system, particularly informal ones, that are not so clear, but play a powerful role in influencing your system's behaviour. These informal rules are the assumptions that rule the personal systems of the humans operating within your system. Assumptions are used by the human brain to guide and control its cognitive processes. These types of rules have the potential to add much complexity to even the smallest of systems. This is because assumptions are not coded and are different for every human being operating within your system. The ability to manage and standardise these types of informal rules is an art, which once mastered, as we will see later on, can propel the success and resilience of any human system, whether it is a personal one or a professional one.

To sum up, effective systems are built on the foundation of well-defined rules, which include policies, procedures, and standards. Policies establish the framework and context to operationalise the purpose of your system while procedures outline, among other things, the step-by-step activities required to implement the policies and to achieve the system's objectives. Standards establish the criteria and benchmarks for the quality and performance of your system's processes and outputs. They focus on promoting excellence within your system. Rules should be used to prescribe specific actions and behaviour only when necessary to ensure compliance and consistency with your processes and their outputs. Altogether, rules allow the humans operating within your system to create the cohesive structure needed to drive operational efficiency and effectiveness, and ultimately, organisational sustainability and success.

Now that you have a deeper understanding what a rule is, the different types of rules used in systems governance and management, and the important role these rules play in the survival of your system, we will now move on to focusing on designing the system you want and need. The next two chapters will provide you guidance on what type of rules to establish and how you can use the rules established as a tool, or lever, to grow your system and build its resilience.

CHAPTER 7

Standardising the Processes That Work Well in Your System

> *The law that entropy always increases—the second law of thermodynamics—holds, I think, the supreme position among the laws of nature.*
> **—Arthur Eddington**

In the first part of this book, you were introduced to the concept of entropy and its role in establishing equilibrium in natural and man-made systems. As you will see later in this chapter, standardisation is a key tool used to control the level of entropy within a system. Nothing is static, even if it appears to be so on the macroscopic level. Change takes place constantly through the movement of photons, electrons, and other basic elements of matter. This change naturally trends towards increasing entropy. In other words, the natural movement of photons, electrons, and atoms—all the basic components that we humans and everything else in this universe are made of—is organically driven by a need to gain increased disorder. In less "chaotic" terms, all the basic components of matter, living and non-living, are organically driven towards gaining the maximum degrees of freedom possible. This natural phenomenon has served us well throughout our evolution.

However, when it comes to driving the effective performance of man-made systems, this phenomenon can be a pain, as without standardisation and stabilisation (stabilisation will be discussed in the subsequent chapter) of the system's processes, we humans will find it extremely difficult to control the processes within our systems. This lack of control could have a disastrous impact on the performance of a system, resulting in the failure of the system to achieve its purpose and the objectives that we have set. The point is that we must institute some measures, such as process standardisation and stabilisation, to mitigate the impact of this natural phenomenon of trending towards higher levels of disorder within a system. If we fail to do so, the result will be a system with less energy being available for use to do the activities we want to do within our system.

Process standardisation and process stabilisation are necessary to limit the level of disorder or entropy within your system. However, before delving deeper into process standardisation in this chapter, I think it is necessary to differentiate disorder from speed. In dealing with standardisation-related matters over the past 2.5 decades, I have found that the two terms, speed and disorder, are often misunderstood and erroneously used interchangeably. This misunderstanding has frequently caused a push-back in the uptake of process standardisation and stabilisation activities in organisational systems governed and managed by the more innovative and entrepreneurial thinking humans.

ALISON S. FOSTER, Ph.D.

Disorder versus Speed

Chapter 3 introduced the concept of speed in relation to the need to control the interactions of your system, both within its internal and external environments, using the braking system of a fast car as an example. Speed is measured as movement in one specific direction as a function of time, and you want your system's processes to be agile, with its processes demonstrating an ability to change at a fast rate. As mentioned earlier, although it may feel counterintuitive, to do so, you need stronger controls if you aim to achieve the fastest possible rate of change in the direction you want your processes to go.

On the other hand, disorder is measured as a function of the degree of freedom experienced by the elements within your system's process. The degree of freedom referred to here is based on the number of directional options that the activities within your processes have. The greater the number of options of directions to go in, the more disorder your system will have. This is exactly what you want to minimise, and you can only do so by standardising your processes.

Therefore, a key takeaway here is that efficient and effective process standardisation, which we will delve deeper into in this chapter, will not impact the speed of your processes, but rather, the disorder, or entropy, associated with your processes.

In addition, coded information, which was explained earlier to refer to documented information, is crucial to and integrally linked with standardisation. You would have realised by now that "information" in its various forms is discussed in several parts of this book. However, in my experience, I have found its misunderstanding to be a major deterrent for both entrepreneurial and non-entrepreneurial leaders of organisational systems when they engage in process standardisation initiatives and activities. Though consultants are usually called in to assist with these types of activities, I think it is important to spend a short time dedicated to explaining the different types of information used in process standardisation, so that organisational leaders can not only engage more effectively with these consultants, but they too can develop an appreciation of the importance of the type and quality of information required and used to standardise their processes.

Types of Data and Information

The energy that flows through the movement of the basic components of matter results in the flow of information through your system. The way in which this energy or information is received and interpreted is determined by how its recipient, human or non-human, is designed to receive and interpret this information. Based on Aristotle's traditional framework, in human systems, the energy flowing from external sources is received as information by humans, via the five primary senses, which are sight, hearing, taste, smell, and touch. However, based on modern science, we know that humans can also receive information intuitively through senses beyond the five primary senses, which includes balance and specialised senses such as magnetic feel detection. For the purpose of this book, however, we will focus on the transmission of information via language because, to date, this form of information transfer has been, and is still the most developed and accepted means of communication throughout humankind.

Words, both spoken and written, serve as an important medium through which information is transferred between humans. Our brain interprets the information we receive through sight, hearing, or for the visually impaired, through braille. Though psychologists and neuroscientists regard the interpretation of words or language as highly subjective, words remain the best means of standardising the flow of information between humans within human systems. This information could be of one of two types—primary or secondary data—and is transferred in various forms.

The basic purest type of information is primary data. Similar to a primary source, primary data is in its original form as collected directly from the source, usually in a binary format. That is, it is described by established units of measurement, in space and time dimensions. To make sense of this type of data, after it is collected, it should be cleaned by removing, among other things, any data points that cannot be explained by common causes. This must be done before any data is analysed. We will delve more into common and special causes in the subsequent chapter, because the ability to differentiate between the two is critical to making sound decisions that are based on measurement. For now, it is sufficient to know that the activities related to analysing data lead to the second type of information, called secondary data.

Similar to a secondary source, secondary data is the product of the analysis of primary data. The quality of this product, the secondary data, depends on the quality of the metadata. Metadata, in this context, refers to the information about the primary data available to the analyser, whether it is a human or an information technology tool. Put another way, metadata refers to information about information, which is valuable to assist the analyser in the analysis of the primary data. Secondary data has its value, as it is cheaper to access through published reports, books, and research papers. However, its accuracy and relevance to solving problems within a system should be guarded and carefully evaluated for many reasons, two of which will be highlighted below.

The first reason is its timeliness. While both types of data are time sensitive, that is, based on past events, despite current innovations within the information communication technology sector attempting to overcome this, by the time the secondary data is published, its information is historic.

The second issue with secondary data is the level of subjectivity associated with it. This subjectivity is inescapable, as it is almost impossible to entirely remove the bias of the author from their words in reporting on the analysis of the data. Even when artificial intelligence has been used to analyse data, the coding to drive and determine what it produces has been written by humans. Besides, artificial intelligence also utilises secondary data in its analysis, so it is almost impossible to eliminate the human impact on data.

Since our brains are designed to analyse information based on past experiences, the result of the interpretation of primary data by two humans with vastly different past experiences could never be the same. This lies at the heart of the business case for the application of diversity and equity policies within organisational systems. Good diversity and equity policies that are implemented well, will enable organisational systems to access vastly different perspectives and interpretations of primary data. Alternative views are exactly what the system needs to make sound predictions on the way forward; And is exactly what planning is about.

In the first part of the book, when we discussed the transfer of information through feedback loops, we saw that all data used for planning is time sensitive. Therefore, sound predictions that determine which direction you should drive your system's processes require, as much as possible, real-time information. Since secondary data could never be a source of real-time information, your system cannot rely only on this type of information. To ensure that your system receives real-time information to influence it to respond the way you want it to, it must be designed with feedback loops that allow your system to receive important data or information on its own, with minimum delay and interference. In other words, your system must be designed with the capacity to collect and harness its own primary data, unique to its own processes. When the information you use to standardise and improve your processes is obtained in this way, you now have a lever which can be used to differentiate your organisational system from that of your competitors within the market. It is therefore important not to waste opportunities to gather information through feedback loops.

I understand, however, this may be easier said than done. With the limited capacity of the human brain to process information, how do you know what data is important for your system to learn and what is not?

The answer to this question lies at the heart of the need to standardise your processes. When dealing with systems, the main purpose of standardisation of anything, whether it is a product or your processes, is to control what information is transferred between processes within the system and between different sub-systems within your overall organisational system. It is impossible to obtain standardisation without the transfer of information, and equally impossible, is the ability to standardise anything in the absence of information.

Standardisation

Standardisation is a critical asset for the human being who is charged with the responsibility of directing and controlling the processes within your system. In the absence of standardised processes, the director or controller, or any human operating within your system, would simply be bombarded with too much information, as the system's processes will naturally generate information, whether there is standardisation or not. With so much information being thrown at humans operating in a system with processes that are not standardised, they will not be able to differentiate noise or useless information, from information that is necessary to inform critical decision-making to steer the system in the direction intended. This could result in the humans within your system zoning out, as the brain's capacity to simulate all this information is maxed out, being wasted on processing unnecessary information. This information overload can be manifested either by disinterest among humans within your system, leading to a lack of or poor decision-making when there is a need to make decisions. Either way, lack of standardised processes within a system can lead to disastrous outcomes for the organisational system over time.

The absence of standardised processes is common in newly established organisational systems, as most of these systems require a mature architecture to support standardisation. Notwithstanding, we know that the age of a system does not equate to its maturity level. I have interacted with many legacy systems, particularly within the developing country context, that do not have defined processes with clear assignments of responsibilities and process owners to control and direct the system's processes. I am sure you too, may have experienced systems like these, at some point in your life. There is a well-known anecdote, of unknown origin, that demonstrates this very well. It is a story involving four people in an organisational system. These humans were called Everybody, Somebody, Anybody and Nobody, and it goes like this:

*There was an important job to be done, and **Everybody** was sure that **Somebody** would do it. **Anybody** could have done it, and **Nobody** did it. **Somebody** got angry about that because it was **Everybody's** job. **Everybody** thought **Anybody** could do it, but he didn't do it, and **Nobody** realised that **Everybody** wouldn't do it. It ended up that **Everybody** blamed **Somebody** when **Nobody** did what **Anybody** could have done.*

This story describes the hallmark of a system without standardised processes.

Informal Systems

We know that a system always exists in its organic form, whether it is informal or formal. When the system is without standardised processes, it is described as informal. Informal systems exhibit at least one of or all three types of control mechanisms:

1. The system's processes are controlled by only one person, the appointed top manager or the owner of the system, who is also the operator. The owner of the system has little time to focus on strategic matters, and there is an absence of independent assurance processes, as the same person is involved in all decision-making and execution/operating processes.

2. A few pseudo-controllers arise. That is, those without the formal authority to control are the ones that appear to be in control. In these cases, the top manager or owner eventually feels like they have lost control over

the system and its processes. Employees are uncertain as to who is really "in charge".

3. The third scenario of control in informal organisational systems is a perception by humans within and outside the system that no one is in control. They believe that the system's processes are not being steered in the direction of its purpose, but rather, the system is moving in all directions, based on whatever information is received.

How can you avoid any of the above scenarios from happening to your system? We established earlier that standardisation involves the control of the flow of information within the system and that information is interpreted by the human brain. Before we delve even deeper into standardisation and how to standardise your processes, we need to first have an appreciation of how the brain interprets the information it receives from the system.

The Psychology of the Human System

Through advancements in the neuroscience field, we now know that the human brain has evolved to function in a very structured manner through modular patterns of thought. This means that the human brain thrives on order by creating patterns based on past experiences, which assist it in interpreting and responding to the external stimuli it receives via in-the-moment transfer of energy or information. Consequently, contrary to nature's yearning for disorder, our brain is designed to crave some level of stability or predictability. This also means that standardisation is a more natural phenomenon to the human brain's thinking system than it is to the natural processes occurring in the environments external to the human body.

Some experts consider this evolutionary track of the human brain to be a "dysfunctional" aspect of the human being, vis-à-vis nature. Notwithstanding, human existence is replete with evidence of the success that can be gained by humans working together to manipulate these internal-external opposing forces by learning how to use standardisation effectively. Standardisation provides a valuable opportunity for balancing nature's opposing interacting forces. In other words, standardisation is a crucial tool that the human being has to help them steer or take control of the direction of a system's processes, which, if left alone, will tend towards complete disorder.

There are several interpretations of standardisation floating across various disciplines. However, because of my familiarity and understanding of the extensively audited consensus-building processes underpinning the international standards development system adopted by the International Organization for Standardization (ISO), my default position is always to reference definitions published by this organisation, wherever they exist. According to the definition published by ISO, standardisation refers to "any activity which establishes provisions for common and repeated use, aimed at achieving the optimum degree of order within a given context". It means, therefore, that if your aim is to counteract nature's forces' trend towards disorder and gain a level of order needed to access useful energy from your system, there is no escaping the need to standardise your system's processes. The useful energy that would be gained from minimising the chaos in your system could then be used to drive your system's processes in the direction that is aligned to the purpose that your system has been established to serve.

At this juncture, it is important, however, to differentiate the difference between standardised processes versus standardised products.

Process vs. Product Standardisation

In my experience, when the term "standardisation" is used in developing countries, it is more often than not associated with standardisation of products and not with standardisation of processes. While the two types of standardisation are related, they are very different, indeed.

In the last chapter we considered processes from the mechanical point of view. That is, unidirectional, progressing in a logical manner from inputs into the process being transformed through activities to create outputs, or products. Product standardisation focuses only on the end product, with the aim of ensuring that it is uniform and of consistent quality. If you are focusing only on the end-product, you are operating solely within the domain of creating and maintaining brand identity, which is based on the perception of your product by its recipients. This is a subject of sub-systems within the marketing and branding domains. The purpose of systems within these domains is to influence the perception of the recipient of your product on its quality, with the hope of increasing the demand for the output of your core processes, driven by the recipients' or potential recipients' want for your system's products.

While the activities within the branding and marketing domains are important, focusing on this external perception without standardising the processes within your system first is a proven recipe for achieving an unsustainable system. Things may appear to be working well for some time, perhaps based on the flow of the energy in your system's external environment, but once anything changes there, your system is at high risk of collapsing.

Consequently, product standardisation should never be a priority and focus before, and definitely without a focus on, process standardisation. My strong view on this matter is not because process standardisation is the area of my experience. There is a plethora of well-documented peer-reviewed published case studies that offer absolutely no shortage of examples of organisational systems that have failed as a result of putting much too much emphasis on issues related to product standardisation, buoyed by marketing and branding experts, before addressing standardisation of the system's internal core and other critical supporting processes.

I personally have also fallen prey to prioritising product over process standardisation with a fruit beverage manufacturing plant I founded several years ago. This was the first of its kind in the Eastern Caribbean sub-region, and I invested a lot of time and money in the cause, which was to create a healthy drink for youngsters from fresh fruit. The idea was great, and the initiative seemed to be going great—designed for compliance with internationally accepted standards for quality and food safety management. It was so great that it attracted the attention of a massive marketing sub-regional company, and I was wooed into going into partnership with that entity. Headed by humans driven by marketing and branding as their core purpose, attention was diverted to "image", at the expense of putting the systems in place necessary to support process standardisation and stabilisation, and hence the sustainability of the juice plant. The rest is history—I eventually exited that organisational system, as its purpose was no longer aligned with the purpose of my personal system and that of the initial organisational system I created. Sunsmart Beverages, later known as Sunfresh Beverages, no longer exists.

How can you too avoid this trap? To prevent this from happening to you or anyone in future generations, I believe all marketing and branding courses offered in programmes undertaken by humans in this field ought to include a mandatory training module on systems and thinking in systems. Such teachings have been part of all engineering and pure science programmes for several decades now. So why have they not been included in all social sciences and business programmes by now? The need for exposure to systems theory is particularly important for humans leading and operating within a developing country's context. This is because most of these countries are characterised by limited resources and have traditionally been on the receiving end of instructions for implementing systems, with little input into designing and building their own, more appropriate, systems for growth and sustainability.

Processes are deemed to be standardised only when they have similar known rules to control the direction of the transfer of energy within and between processes within your system. Beware of the presence of similar inputs converted to similar outputs through similar activities within your system. In the absence of rules, even if these conditions exist, it does not mean that the processes within your organisational system are standardised.

You may recall that we established earlier the tendency of nature's processes to trend towards the direction of greatest disorder in order to achieve maximum degrees of freedom. Therefore, without rules to guide the activities within your processes, you will end up wasting a lot of energy, time, and money on product standardisation. This, of course, can never be sustainable. Time is the equalising constraint that all systems have. This is true for your systems, and those of your competitors. Every human in all systems within the domain you are operating has 24 hours in the day. What you choose to do, and to have the humans within your organisational system do, with this time is what will set your business system apart from your competitors.

Standard Operating Procedures

Prioritising the standardisation of your system's internal processes is what will give you an edge. But to do so, you must develop and implement rules unique to your system's internal and external environments. These rules will allow you to have control over your system's processes. Such rules are developed and expressed through formulation of sound, implementable policies and procedures, traditionally referred to as standard operating procedures (SOPs). Procedures were already discussed at length in the preceding chapter, but for re-emphasis, it is important to know that policies and procedures are deemed implementable only when they are expressed and documented in a manner that can be easily communicated between all humans within the system. SOPs can be documented in manuals for operators and converted to handbooks for users of the outputs of the processes identified in the SOP and manual.

Prior to the information and communication technology (ICT) era, these manuals and handbooks were physical documents, which humans within organisational systems referred to when needed. Now, with innovative means of documenting and communicating, attractive and interactive ICT platforms are used to operationalise such manuals through digitised processes. These can be accessed via mobile devices and other media, making it easier for the humans within your system to access the right information, at the right time.

However, for your system's processes to be digitised, you need to first establish appropriate rules to standardise your processes. These rules ought to be documented in a standard format or SOP. Expressing the rules that you create in a well-documented manner, using SOPs, establishes a type of semantic standardisation for your system. Semantic standardisation allows for a common understanding of the meaning of the words used by all humans within your system and ought to be a prerequisite to attempts to standardise your processes. Words or language influence human beliefs, and beliefs influence the mindset, which in turn influences human actions and behaviour. This will ultimately be what reflects the culture of your human organisational system. A very strong correlation has been established between the culture of an organisational system and the quality of a system's decision-making processes.

The Case for Process Standardisation

In this era of information technology, digital transformation is too often used as the sole driver for process standardisation, instead of the other way around. The sole purpose of process standardisation should never be for digitisation. The benefits of process standardisation have been known for centuries, long before we even developed language to describe it and much longer before the first computing device was ever established. Therefore, the goal should be to pursue process standardisation to achieve its inherent benefits for your system's sustainability, using ICT as a tool to implement effective and efficient process standardisation. Once you truly understand and appreciate this, your digital transformation efforts will lead to huge benefits.

Of all the benefits process standardisation offers, predictability of the behaviour of your system's processes stands at the top of my list. Why? Because if your processes are standardised, you, as the manager, owner, or director, have more flexibility to pay attention to the more strategic aspects of your business or other organisational system.

We know that the human brain has limited capacity to process information. Though the level of capacity varies from human to human, as it is based on an individual's genetics and environmental factors, the capacity of all human brains is limited, full stop. Like computers, our brains must stop working periodically to be re-charged through rest, sleep, and other means. If it does not do this, it loses its ability to process information in a logical manner. Therefore, in order to direct and manage any system effectively and efficiently, whether it is an organisational one or a personal one, you need to be sure that you make effective use of the limited brain space and capacity that it has and prioritise the information it receives. This is especially important for systems with vertical centralisation of decision-making authorities.

More importantly, when you design your system to operate with standardised processes, you are ensuring that you or your directors and managers can focus on the information that is needed, with minimal noise or distraction, affording everyone the brain space to pay attention to strategy formulation and implementation—activities which are critical for the sustainability of all human systems.

Another inescapable driver for process standardisation is the role it plays in facilitating the scalability of your system. If your organisational system starts off small, like entrepreneurial ventures ought to do, chances are you may not want to have your business system remain small. Rather, you would want to grow your system, increasing its capacity to produce more, in order to meet a growing demand. To do this, you must replicate your processes while maintaining the level of quality of your product and service that your early recipients would have grown to expect. Whether or not you digitise and use artificial intelligence, replication often, and inevitability requires the introduction of more humans into the system.

For example, it would be impossible to maintain the same level of quality of customer service when you started a business with three customers, and your business then suddenly grew to 300 customers. When you had three customers, it is more than likely you were personally involved in both the production of the goods and interfacing with your customers. However, as your business grew to 300 customers, it would be impossible for you personally to interact with every customer, especially in a timely manner. If you want to ensure that all customers receive the same quality of service, just as you delivered when you had three customers, you will need to invest time and money into developing a customer relationship management (CRM) system. This will require a documented SOP to guide the additional humans you hire or bring into your system to implement and manage its customer relations processes.

With a sound CRM system, supported by your well-documented SOPs, it will be easier to transfer responsibilities, information, or tasks from one person, team, or department to another. When this is backed by digitisation of your processes, you can expect better integration and process continuity. These benefits are particularly useful for organisations that utilise shift systems or those operating in multiple locations.

Process standardisation through the development of appropriate SOPs that are easily accessible to everyone within your system allows for redeployment of humans within your system to different processes. The ability of your organisational system to redeploy the humans operating within it to different processes allows for process continuity, and this is directly correlated with your system's overall continuity over time. If your system is a business system, this is what business continuity is about.

The effects of the COVID-19 pandemic provided the business research community with a plethora of data to prove that the businesses that were able to survive the scathing impact of this pandemic were the ones with formalised management systems. That is, these were the business systems with processes that were already standardised and well documented. If you are an owner or operator of a system, you need to look no further for evidence to be convinced of the tremendous value of process standardisation to your system's sustainability.

Alignment

For process standardisation to be effective, it must be aligned to the system's core purpose and strategy for development. In addition, process standardisation ought to be supported by just enough structure to facilitate interactions or the flow of the right information in both vertical and horizontal directions. Too much structure within a system creates calcification. You want to avoid this at all costs, as it clogs the channels through which information flows and limits your system's ability to adapt. Just the right amount of structure, though, allows for access to the right information needed for good decision-making to continuously nourish and fulfil the purpose of the human system you created whilst allowing it to be flexible enough to adapt to changes within its internal and external context. Alignment of your processes to the purpose of your system is particularly important as the humans within your system are also a part of several other systems, each with its own purpose.

Despite what anyone may cause you to believe, of all the systems that humans belong to, the purpose of their personal system is the one that competes for the human brain's attention over the purpose of any other system the human may be a part of. This may sometimes be referred to as the animal or human instinct for survival. To complicate things further, no two personal systems can ever be the same, as each one is based on the qualia and quanta of human experiences, which are processed in a very subjective manner. Since values drive the way humans behave, once your processes are designed in a manner to align with your organizational system's values, and these values are aligned with the values of the humans operating within your system, the positive impact of process standardisation on operational efficiency and effectiveness will be the highest.

Notwithstanding all of the above, it is natural for humans to err. Often these errors can have a major impact on the quality of the endpoint produced. Process standardisation will provide you with a framework within which your system can operate. Once this framework is established, you can implement a monitoring and evaluation system to measure the performance of your system's processes over time. This allows you to institute the checks and balances needed to stabilise and control the processes within your system.

In the next chapter, we will delve deeper into why when you stabilise your processes and you have appropriate control over them, you are better able to introduce changes for improvement. Counter-intuitively, the art of creating less disorder within your system through process standardisation increases the agility of your system.

On a final note for this chapter, I believe that learning the art of process standardisation is extremely fulfilling, as only when you go through the process of standardising your system's processes, do you truly get to know the system you created and you are a part of.

CHAPTER 8

Stabilising Your Standardised Processes

Understanding variation is the key to success in quality and business.
—**Sir W.E. Deming**

At this stage, you should be aware of the processes at work within your system, and you hopefully have realized the need for standardised processes. You should have also realized the need to set some rules to control your processes. Once these are implemented you may think at this point, everything should be okay because you have established the rules needed to control your processes and scale your system.

But is everything really okay? Should you now expect the standardised processes within your system to be automatically stabilised? The simple answer to these questions is no. Absolutely not.

The assurance of stability certainly cannot be gained so easily. Though "stability" may look like nothing is happening from the outside, it takes some continual action on the inside to get visible stability on the outside. In systems theory, a process can be described as stable only if the humans within the system can predict the behaviour of its processes over time. You would recall that the basic elements of all systems are in constant motion, always seeking to gain maximum entropy. This means that the elements within the personal systems of each human in your human system are constantly in motion too, continuously changing to find the maximum degree of freedom whilst being buttressed by the individual's sense of mental order. What this means in practice is that setting the rules for the processes within your system is meaningless if you do not have a plan of action to monitor and control your processes, using the rules that you have set for guidance. If your desire is to be in control of your system's growth and sustainability, you must have a plan to manage the processes within your system.

While your personal system includes interactions and interdependences between the personal systems of other humans and that of different organisational systems, your personal system really includes only one human being, and one human mind—and that is yours. So, the rules and standards that govern most of the processes within your personal system need little, if any, codification (documentation) for you to gain control of your personal system's processes. You may choose to codify the rules you wish to apply to some of your processes to serve as a constant reminder and to gain the benefits associated with visualisation techniques. However, codification of rules may be only necessary for standardisation of the processes within your personal system if you are not in control of this system, which hopefully is not the case. It may also be necessary if you share control of your personal system with someone else. Most people seem quite happy to share control of some processes within their personal system with at least one partner, as it may get quite complex and energy draining to co-control personal processes effectively and efficiently with multiple partners.

Many strive to gain control over all the processes within their personal system. Some may describe this state as utopia, as it is impossible to be solely in control of all your processes. Nevertheless, I believe it is worth striving to be in control of all the critical processes associated with the survival or sustainability of your personal system. I think the highest priority among these critical personal processes ought to be given to those related to your mental, spiritual, and physical health, as well as your freedom of thought.

Organisational systems are different. Organisations are human systems of varying sizes. These can be micro-, small, medium-sized or big organisations, each serving a different purpose. Irrespective of its size, chances are there are two or more human beings interacting with each other and with the processes within your organisational system. In addition, irrespective of its size, your organisational system may, at any one time, be serving multiple recipients within multiple locations. This means that your services and/or products are being used by multiple consumers at the same time. Therefore, at any one time, you would more than likely have multiple processes within your system, some of which produce the same result or output, and others serving different purposes, but related to the same output of your core processes.

As seen in the previous chapter, it is always much easier to manage multiple processes if these processes are standardised. When managing systems, a process is deemed to be standardised when the same rules apply to the same processes within the system. These rules can include using the same control limits to guide your decision-making as the process manager. A mistake that is often made is to believe that because two processes produce the same output or result, that these two processes are the same or standardised. For instance, if you are a professional service provider, and within your organisational system you have two different secretaries working within your administrative sub-system, both preparing client intake letters (CILs), and these two secretaries adopt an entirely different set of activities to produce the CILs, using different standards and rules, your client intake processes are not standardised. The same product may be produced—the CIL—but there is no guarantee that all CILs will meet the objectives that you have set as the service provider. In such instances, the assumption, that the product is the same and will always be the same, is an error and is often the root cause of much instability within a system.

Although using process standardisation as a tool would bring you the closest you can get to having any two processes behave in the same way, it is impossible for the activities, even within these standardised processes, to behave exactly in the same manner. Activities within a system's processes can exhibit varying behaviour patterns due to several reasons. These reasons may be as a result of both internal and external factors. External factors range from changes in the environment of your system, which are essentially changes within systems external to yours, that are interacting with your system's processes. Internal factors relate to changes with the elements within your system, ranging from equipment, material, financing, and, of course, within the personal systems of the humans operating in your system. Notwithstanding, once your processes are being managed effectively using established rules, which include control limits, your processes could achieve the level of stability that you want, even with the cacophony of activities within them.

Only when your processes are stable, will you be able to predict how they will behave. And only then, you will be in a better position to have effective control over them and direct them in the way you want. Controlling and directing are two different functions. Process control is a management function, which occurs closer to the operations level within your system. Directing, on the other hand, is a governance function and ought not to be confused with management. This is true even when both governance and management processes are being executed by the same human being. Both good governance and management are crucial for optimising the performance of your system. In the final part of this book, we will delve deeper into process direction or the governance function, which involves effective strategy formulation to generate the value of your system in a manner that can be utilised by the recipients of your products and services.

But first, it is important that you understand how to manage your processes to achieve stability and control. This art of management is critical for the sustainability of all human systems. When management of your processes is done well, you will know when and how to respond when you observe variation in the behaviour of processes within your system. It is only when you respond at the right time, with the right actions, that your system can be described as being stable. Achieving stability at the process level is where all control changes within your system take place.

Control Limits

How do you know what changes or variations in your processes you need to be concerned about? And how do you know what action you should take when you do decide to act? First, you need to know what to look for at the process level within your system. That is, you need to decide what indicators, or rather, what activities within your processes, result in an attribute that can be observed or measured. Already activities within processes in your system are invisible to the human eye, so the indicators chosen to be monitored ought to be capable of being measured and described accurately by a metric, and upper and lower acceptable limits of this metric must be established. These upper and lower acceptable measurements are what you refer to as your "control limits".

For instance, if you are operating a food manufacturing plant producing pasteurised milk drinks for human consumption, you will need to set control limits for the temperature of the milk whilst it is being processed. These upper and lower temperature limits will be guided by scientific evidence of the temperature range at which the milk should be maintained in order to avoid spoilage due to microbial growth. Alternatively, if you are running a service business, and your promise to the recipient of your services is a specified time period for processing their complaints, you will need to establish a set of time control limits for the activities within the processes that belong to your complaints management system. The time for conducting these activities ought to be monitored closely, and the results will serve as an indicator for you to determine whether your complaints management system is meeting the objectives set and serving the purpose of your organisational system.

For your personal system, your control limits will be influenced by your values, cultural norms, or desires related to where you want to be in life. For your organisational system, your governing body, in conjunction with the senior management team, ought to set these control limits guided by lessons learnt from its own mistakes in the past, experiments, and industry standards or best practices.

When you have established the average value of the metric that describes the indicator you have chosen, and you have set its upper and lower acceptable limits, you need to ensure that the process indicator that you have established is monitored and measured over time to determine how the process activities are behaving.

There is an entire body of knowledge which provides guidance on how to establish appropriate control limits. This body of knowledge rests within the statistical process control (SPC) domain, and there are several experts out there who can help you establish these, depending on the industry you are in. Based on what is at stake for you and your system, you may wish to hire a statistician or scientist to assist you with setting your process control limits. But for the most part, especially if the organisational system you are responsible for is not operating within a highly regulated space, with the help of an independent person who appreciates systems management, you should be okay. At KMA Consulting, we are always thrilled to assist organisations that need help in this area. When it comes to your personal system, however, perhaps all you need is to take the necessary time to pause and reflect.

The level of rigidity you would like to have in your processes would determine the spread of your control limits. For high-precision processes, such those used to produce medical devices and IT equipment, a narrower spread of control limits is required. Notwithstanding, your processes should be designed to ensure that their activities are controlled in a manner that ensures that the measurements of your chosen process indicators are kept as close as possible to your average or mean targeted value. These measurements should be taken during operation and plotted on a control chart or process behaviour chart over time.

An example is shown below of a control chart, which was used to monitor the time taken to produce a civil status certificate, from the point at which one is requested. The chart shows the average time taken to produce the civil status certificate plotted over a period of 15 days, with the X or horizontal axis reflecting days within the first half of month, and the Y or vertical axis reflecting the average number of days taken to produce the certificate requested on the specified day.

Control Chart / Process Behaviour Chart

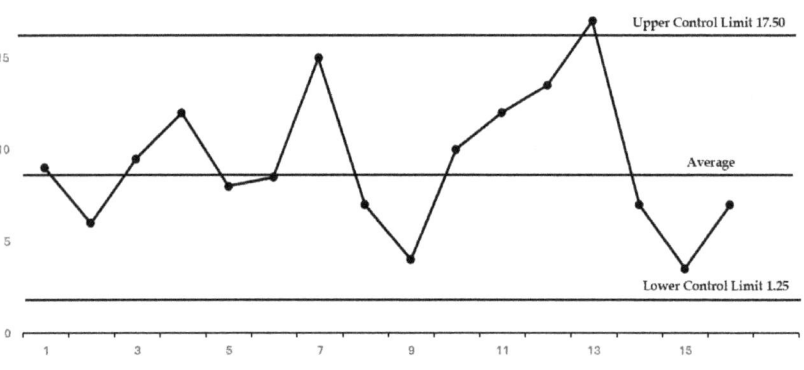

Most of the time, if the measurements for your control limits are well considered, researched, and validated, the spread of the indicator's measurements taken over time would be even, on either side of the average targeted value, with all of the data points lying within the upper and lower control limits. Once this is the case, the measurements taken should remain within the upper and lower control limits, and any deviation from the targeted mean should not be a surprise, as this deviation would be deemed to be due to natural variation or "common causes". For instance, the human operator may not have been feeling well at the time or due to some other random cause. In such cases, there would be no need to take any action to change anything or activity within your process.

In the case of the above example with the civil status certificate, it is clear that the managers or directors of the organisational system established a quality service standard of not more than 15 days, plus or minus 1, for the production of the certificate. Based on the chart, it is evident that this target was met for all of the first 15 days of the month, except in one instance, on the 13th day, when the average time was more than 15 days.

If, however, you observe that the indicator's measurement has gone above or below the upper or lower limits, this should initiate some concern, as this may be due to a special cause. In the example demonstrated above, this special cause may have been due to a shortage of staff because one of the workers fell ill. If your investigation determined this to be the cause of the variation, then the manager may want to ensure that staff in other departments within the organisation that deal with support processes are cross-trained, so that they can be deployed to assist with core processes to compensate for any changes in the human resources in this area.

A special cause may also be at play if your measurements are clustered on only one side of your control chart. In an organisational system where the person monitoring the indicator notices this, they need to bring this to the attention of the process owner or process manager.

It should be noted that if the observation of the indicator falling outside the control limits occurs frequently, a root cause analysis would need to be undertaken to determine the source or root cause of this error. The findings of this analysis should inform the decision that management would need to take at the operational level to correct this from recurring. On a more strategic level, the results of the root cause analysis ought to be used to guide senior management and the governing body on what decisions ought to be taken and what new measures need to be invested in to prevent this type of error from occurring.

However, be mindful that the results of the root cause analysis do not provide proof of a causal relationship between the factors identified and the observation made. This is because root cause analysis utilises investigative, non-experimental techniques. Only with the use of experimental techniques such as randomised control trials or laboratory experiments can you arrive at the closest point to establishing causal relationships between factors and indicators. It is advisable to engage the skills of an independent consultant, who can use experimental and non-experimental methods to guide you in the development of your strategy, policies, and procedures for improving the performance of the processes within your organisational system. They can also assist you in ensuring that your decision-making processes are risk-based and modeled on systems thinking.

Indicators

You do not need to plot control charts for all your processes. In some cases, you may need none. However, irrespective of the type of system you are dealing with, the principles of effective process control are the same. Whatever the size of your system and whatever purpose it serves, you need to establish what indicators you will be monitoring to give you a clue or signal of the behaviour of your system's process. These indicators could be qualitative or quantitative. A qualitative indicator is a non-numerical measure used to assess characteristics, quality, or perceptions of the user or recipient of the process output. Examples include the level of employee satisfaction or user satisfaction the product produced.

On the other hand, a quantitative indicator is a numerical measure, such as employee turnover rate, which is calculated by dividing the number of employees who left the organisation within a specified period by the total number of employees within the organisation, and multiplying this by 100. As we saw in the first part of this book, qualitative indicators are more subjective than quantitative indicators, as they are based on the perception of the human observer. While surveys can be used as a tool for assessing the performance of the processes within your system, and their analysis involves the use of quantitative measures, the responses are still considered opinionated, due to the effect of the human qualia discussed earlier.

Whether or not you intend to use control charts to monitor your processes, it will help you control your processes if you develop a mindset aligned with the general principles of process management for everything you do. The same is true for everything you are in control of in your daily life. It is only when you are able to control your processes that you are able to steer them in the direction you want them to go.

We have seen earlier that to be able to move fast in a specified direction, you need strong controls and a good braking system, just like the fastest cars have. In living systems, which is exactly what human systems are, the capacity of the human brain to master the ability to design and implement strong control mechanisms is an important skill. This skill has enabled humankind to balance and harness energy from entropy, and it is what has placed us in a class of our own, on top of the food chain in the animal kingdom. So, let us use this given capacity to build resilience into our systems.

Be extremely careful with your choice of indicators and consequently what you monitor. Choose process indicators that make sense and that you know you can monitor and measure. A good process indicator will provide meaningful, actionable, or accurate information about a process. It should be relevant, specific, measurable, and aligned with the desired outcomes. A bad process indicator could lead to unintended consequences. For example, if you want to monitor the performance of your human resource development team, tracking the number of staff training sessions held and attended would be a poor indicator, as this does not give information on whether the training was effective and whether the employees gained new skills and knowledge.

To make sense, your process indicator must help you to predict the behaviour of your processes and help you distinguish unnecessary noise from real issues, so that you do not waste time on frivolous matters due to common causes. In other words, process indicators with good control limits will guide you on what information or observations you should ignore and what you should pay attention to. The indicators that you choose ought to help you to develop and maintain the sustainability of your system, whether it is personal or organisational.

Your process indicators should, therefore, be linked and aligned with indicators that determine whether your system is fulfilling its purpose and whether the strategy for doing so is being implemented in an effective manner. If your process indicators are not aligned to these higher strategic objectives, you will be wasting time measuring the wrong things. It means that you would be receiving the wrong information to guide your decision-making processes. In systems management lingo, this is the garbage-in-garbage-out effect, with a high risk of decisions taken, resulting in disastrous outcomes.

For instance, if you are running a service organisation, and you want to track the quality of your customer service, it would be useless to measure only the length of time your employees spend on calls with customers. This might lead to your staff rushing calls to reduce the time spent with the customer or purposefully and unnecessarily making calls last quite a long time, as either of these would compromise the quality of customer service and customer satisfaction.

In addition, pay attention to the use of high-level indicators that focus on monitoring the impact of strategic decisions. These indicators are referred to as key performance indicators (KPIs), and they serve the purpose of reporting to parties external to your system. They say nothing about the level of control or stability of your processes. To be in control of your system and have the capacity to steer it in the direction you want it to go, you need to establish monitoring and reporting mechanisms at the process level. This level is too often relegated as being just "operational" and operates in silos, separate and apart from management and governance processes. With a true systems-thinking mindset, there will be the appropriate level of integration of these processes into your decision-making processes at the management and governance levels.

Care must also be taken to establish and monitor process indicators that provide information regarding negative reinforcing loops, which were discussed earlier in this book. Your ability to choose these indicators and manage them carefully is critical for preventing outcomes that are catastrophic for the survival and sustainability of your system.

With a better appreciation of how systems work (the subject of Part 1), and an idea of how to direct and control the performance of your processes (the subject of Part 2) , we will now move on to the final part of this book, which will bring you much closer to achieving the aim of the book: developing a strategy for thinking-in-systems and for building resilience into your system, whether it is a personal one or an organisational one.

PART III

THE ART OF BUILDING RESILIENCE

CHAPTER 9

What Does a Resilient System Look Like?

> *The most stunning thing living systems can do is to change themselves utterly by creating whole new structures and behaviours. In biological systems that power is called evolution.*
> —**Donella H. Meadows**

To understand what makes a system resilient, we need to first go back to the fundamental property of systems, a characteristic of systems that is non-negotiable. This fixed property is described as holism. In the first part of this book, we spent some time explaining this key characteristic of systems, which is associated with the term "holistic". When described this way, it means that the whole, i.e., the system, is greater and much more complex than the simple sum of its parts can ever be. For the purpose of this book, resilience and sustainability are terms always used with reference to an entire system, even when that system exists as a sub-system within a larger system. With this perspective, the focus suddenly becomes on the outcome of all the interactions within the system, which bears on the system's ability to continuously serve its purpose.

This is an important philosophical underpinning of systems thinking. Resilience and sustainability are goals that are never established only with reference to the parts of a system or its sub-systems. When adopting a system's mindset, or a systems approach to solving problems, always ensure that the whole is remains the focus—without fail. Remember, this "whole" is in reference to the purpose the system was created to serve. Too often, policy- and other decision-makers within organisational systems, and in our personal systems as well, spend too much time focusing on narrow, reductionist-type methods, such as investigative processes. In addition, too often, resilience-building efforts are focused on only one or a few parts of the system to the detriment of other parts within the system. This approach ultimately redounds to the detriment of the sustainability of the entire system. If we continue with only a narrow reductionist approach to solving our problems, our system will fail to continue to fulfil its purpose—the essence of what the system was created for.

Before we delve deeper into the discussion of resilience from a system's perspective, it is necessary to differentiate the concept of "growth" from that of "resilience". These two terms are quite different and are too often used mistakenly in an interchangeable manner. I believe that this misunderstanding more often than not lies at the heart of poor decision-making in both organisational and personal systems, and results in short-term gains with disastrous outcomes for the sustainability of the overall system.

Growth

In entomological terms, the word "growth" precedes that of "resilience", by over three centuries. It is, therefore, not surprising that in the English language, the word "growth" connotes a more limiting concept compared to the meaning embodied by "resilience". While growth is loosely used to refer to the process of increasing in size, value, or level of the complexity of the general significance of a system, it is usually linked to only a specific indicator that is based on measurements of one or a few attributes or characteristics of the system. The change in this indicator is monitored over a specific period of time to determine whether it is increasing, decreasing, or staying the same over that specified time period. The attribute chosen to be monitored and measured to determine whether the system is growing or reducing must, therefore, be easy to measure. Its relationship to the system's other components and other attributes of the system ought to be well understood.

Only when the attribute is easy to measure and its relationship with other components within the system is well understood can the measurements taken or data collected be useful for determining the overall behaviour patterns of the system. The attribute, however, must be continuously monitored at a set frequency, and the data obtained from its measurements must be continuously analysed at specified intervals.

Growth means different things in different contexts, and so the indicators for growth vary depending on the context. For instance, biological growth usually means an increase in physical size or maturation over time, as seen in organisms or cells, while personal growth involves the improvement or development of personal qualities, skills, or perspectives, often tied to achieving goals or fulfilling potential. Business growth, on the other hand, often means expanding operations, increasing revenue, profits, or market share, and scaling operations sustainably while economic growth refers to an increase in the economic output of a country, typically measured as a rise in gross domestic product (GDP). One would expect that the latter would usually give an indication of higher productivity, more employment, and improved standards of living, but this is not always the case. So, our social scientists may argue that social growth indicators, such as the progress and advancement in societal structures, social relations, or standards of living, are more important than pure economic growth indicators.

The analysis of the data associated with monitoring growth needs great care, and must be done always with the view that one data point means nothing unless it is considered within a reasonable set of good quality data points. In addition, understand that while the function of data collection could be delegated, the total responsibility of analysing the data ought never to be devolved from the humans within the system, who are accountable for the overall performance of the system, even when assisted by artificial intelligence. Why?

To begin with, analysing the growth of any system is a complex matter and depends on what targets are set for the system. These targets are usually set by those accountable for the system, and so these targets are better understood by the humans who set them. Also, commitment to achieving targets has been demonstrated to be greatest among those who have been part of the process of establishing them. Moreover, the value of the growth indicator to building resilience is not directly proportional to its ease of measurement. The relationship is usually extremely complex, and in many cases, relies on unmeasurable attributes. Some of these attributes include intuition or gut feelings, trust between team members, or other fuzzy attributes, difficult to measure.

Whatever it is, when the analysis and evaluation of data or metrics taken from the system is carried out by humans with a mindset removed from the lower altitudes of doing work within the system, the results are usually better aligned to building resilience of that system. This is a defining factor that distinguishes resilient systems from non-resilient systems that demonstrate growth over a specified period of time. When humans with the capacity to think at the higher altitude, that is the level at which strategy formulation takes place, and these humans are also the ones accountable for the performance of the system's processes and analysing and evaluating the growth metrics, the chances for building a resilient system would always be much better. There may be many reasons for this, but one of the reasons I think that is often overlooked is that these are the humans within the system that usually have the security and the psychological safety to infuse the less measurable fuzzy, but needed attributes, such as intuition and gut feeling, into the decision-making processes.

Growth indicators, like all other indicators, are time sensitive—some to a greater extent than others. In addition, the value of an indicator is only as good as the stability of the processes within the internal environment of the system and that of the environment external to the system. However, we know that energy is fluid, constantly moving and changing the media through which it moves. This results in an ever-changing environment, both within the internal and external context of the system you are responsible for. It stands to reason, therefore, that your indicators may not be telling you the same story that they had been telling you a year ago, or even a month ago, depending on the rate of change of the internal and external environments of your system.

Economic and social theorists have attempted to standardise and establish benchmarks for rates of change within certain sectors and industries, some of which your organizational system may belong to. Whilst these benchmarks may be useful to inform academic-like activities often associated with the engagement of certain types of consultancy services, it is important that you, personally, periodically test the validity of the indicators you are using to inform the performance of your system, for yourself. This is because no external domain expert can fully experience the type of changes that are taking place within and around the system you are a part of on a daily basis. Therefore, the pace at which you can detect these changes would always be faster than that of any external consultant.

In addition, try always to avoid falling into the trap of relying blindly on comparisons of data from your system against measurements of similar indicators used in other systems. We all fall into this trap at some point in our lives, not just on the organisational system's level, but also the personal system level. As I write this, it is with a deep heart. With three young-adult daughters, I am keenly aware how challenging it is to avoid the temptation of comparing our personal system with that of other humans. The use of social media has made access to information about other personal systems so easy. But as we saw earlier, no two systems are the same, and this holds true for both organisational and personal systems. When the internal and external environments of any two human systems are different, the indicators used to judge the success of one personal system cannot be the same for another.

We established earlier that the human brain is designed to look for patterns, and it thrives on "order". So, it is not surprising that there will be a tendency to believe that the measurements of your indicator can be interpreted in the same way as that of a similar indicator for another system. But too often this could lead to making hasty decisions based on a comparison of results of indicators with no consideration of the differences between the internal and external context of the different systems that each is associated with. Try your best to resist this tendency at all costs. If your aim is to ensure the sustainability of your system, it would definitely be worth taking the time and energy to counter this tendency of comparison and focus on what the data of your system is telling you, based on your understanding of its own internal and its external context, and not that of other systems.

Resilience

Systems experts know that indicators of growth are never a good measure of how resilient the system is. In fact, it is well established that if a system or any of its sub-systems is growing too quickly, at a pace that is faster than the pace at which its internal structure can reorganise itself, the system would either explode or implode, making it impossible for it to continue to serve its true purpose. You would recall that a system's structure is really made up of the interactions within the system through which information flows. While it is necessary to control the flow of information for many reasons which were discussed earlier, if the interactions within the system's sub-systems are limited, it would take a much longer time for the structure of the system to change. These types of limitations make it impossible for the internal structure of the overall system to evolve at a fast enough pace to keep up with the growth of other parts of the system that are receiving information from the outside quickly and responding to it organically.

So, understand this, the most resilient system is one that has an internal structure that is flexible enough to allow it to reorganise itself spontaneously and freely in a well-distributed manner. This principle underpins the resilience of natural systems in evolutionary theory and is no different for organisational and personal systems, which we, as humans, are all a part of.

There is no doubt that for both organisational and personal systems, you need some extent of structure, especially if your aim is to align the growth of your system with building resilience. Perhaps this is because, as discussed earlier, the natural physical nature of the human brain and thinking system is designed in a manner to function in modular patterns. It is through these structured patterns of the brain that energy flows to give rise to matters of the mind manifested through the intangible—thoughts, feelings, emotions, and everything related to the conscious being. So, it makes sense to put some structure into the physical systems that we belong to—to help the brain process the stimuli or information it receives from the external world.

Be careful with the type of structure you institute. You need only the right amount of structure, not too much structure and not structure that is too rigid. The irony of this is that too much structure restricts the flow of new information into the brain, and this stifles its ability to be creative, to change, and to adapt to changes around it. Therefore, just the right level of structure is needed.

How do you know when you have enough structure—and not too much on one extreme to create rigidity within your system or too little on the opposite extreme to allow for utter chaos? How do you know whether the structure you have is enough? You know when your structure is enough when it allows you some control over the quality of information generated and received, and when you know how this information flows within your system. For instance, we know that the most important sub-system in any organisational system is the personal system belonging to the humans within your system—with no two personal systems being identical. Although often overlooked, I believe these sub-systems are the most important of all the other sub-systems within the organisational system because humans are the decision-makers of policy and other rules that are designed to control the flow of information and, therefore, the structural architecture of your system.

This means that humans within your system, collectively, and in some cases individually, have the power to influence the nature of the backbone of your system—the very structure that is the key determinant of its resilience. Because of this power, I think it is important to spend some time delving a little deeper into the relationship between the human's personal system and the overall structure of your organisational system that human beings belong to. This, in turn, would determine your system's resilience.

The Personal System

It is well established that our actions are influenced by our belief system—a system which includes a set of principles and tenets that form the basis of our understanding of the physical world around us. Research in the neuroscience field has confirmed that our belief system is determined by the information our brain receives. Further, research has also proven that our belief system will be influenced by any type of information received—whether this information is true or false. In fact, the brain's processes cannot decipher what is true or false. It is simply controlled by the stories the mind tells it.

From a philosophical point of view, this creates the mind-body problem and brings us into the realm of two extremist views: dualism versus physicalism. At one end, dualism treats the mind and body as distinct entities, while physicalism treats everything of the mind as an explanation of physical processes of the brain. Increasingly, modern research is closing the gaps between these two divergent views by conducting research on the effects of thought on the neurological and other physical processes within the human body. The results of this research are increasingly blurring the lines between the philosophical and scientific belief systems and are getting closer to bringing unity between them.

One thing is certain: information, in the form of energy transfer, plays a critical role in how our belief systems, and by extension, our personal system evolves. It is, therefore, critical to ensure that only verified and validated information flows into your personal system. With just the right amount of structure within the organisational system, you can be closer to ensuring that your systems receive only genuine and accurate information. The quality of such information is controlled through verification and validation processes.

Verification and Validation Processes

Verification processes include activities executed to check the correctness of the information. For example, in an organisational system, it may include cross-checking employees names and date of birth, as recorded on their identification cards, against what is documented in their HR records. Validation processes, however, refer to activities that check the fitness for use, or appropriateness of the information, to the context in which it would be used. For instance, a vehicle could be designed and manufactured according to specific safety standards, and the results from testing undertaken during the manufacturing processes could provide verification for this. However, the vehicle's safety can only be validated by the users of the vehicle when the vehicle is used under real-world driving conditions.

In addition to ensuring that the information your system's processes receive is verified and validated, it is important to control how the information flows within your system. The "control" referred to here does not equate to limiting information, but rather controlling its quality and the direction the information flows in through the interactions allowed between the various processes within your system.

Growth and resilience are excellent goals to set and to achieve for your system. However, resilience can only be achieved when the growth of your system is controlled at a pace that allows for the concurrent reorganisation of your system's structure. We saw earlier that your system's processes can be fed with good quality information through robust feedback loops embedded within the system's structure. This provides a fantastic avenue for information flow related to the performance of processes within your system that are not performing satisfactorily. If you become aware that your system is not fulfilling its purpose effectively and efficiently, you can use this information to tweak its processes to bring them back on track. Or you can create drastic changes to the processes within the system, which may include changing the structure of one or more of your system's sub-systems.

In summary, building resilience is all about the capacity of the system to change and to withstand change, both at the broader organisational system level, and within your system's sub-systems, the smallest of which is the personal system. If you only have one take away after reading this book, I hope it is this: a system can only be deemed to be sustainable when its structure is resilient enough to allow its purpose to endure. It is only when the purpose endures beyond the sustainability of the system's sub-systems, stocks, and its other parts that history can confirm the system as being resilient.

In addition, on a personal level, the realisation that your personal system is part of something, a system that is bigger and much greater than itself, puts resilience and sustainability into a whole new perspective. This is why the following chapter, which will provide you with a strategy for building resilience within your organisational system, will focus on an approach that you can use to minimise the impact of the subjective effects of emotions, which are intrinsically linked to personal systems, on the performance of your system's processes.

CHAPTER 10

A Strategy for Building Resilience: Lessons from a Personal Journey

He who has a "why" can endure any "how".
—**Frederick Nietzsche**

What I am about to share with you in this chapter has been informed by not just results of scientific research, but importantly by lessons learnt from my own personal journey, through various life-experiences, from childhood into adulthood, marriage to divorce and marrying again, establishing to winding down various entrepreneurial ventures and assisting with doing the same for some public entities, working with several political and non-political leaders, founder and non-founder chief executives, operational and technical staff, and lastly, but profoundly, raising three beautiful little girls into young ladies, whilst caring for aging parents through to the end of their life-cycles. Though my experience has been largely within a "small island developing state, post-colonisation" context, interacting heavily with regional and international systems, my systems-thinking mind has caused me to notice some common patterns that influence decision-making processes in the evolution of all human systems, irrespective of the context within which they operate.

From childhood, I have been intrigued by why humans make the decisions they make within the systems they operate, irrespective of the purpose of the system. To answer that question, I needed to get a better understanding of how the brain works and the impact of the brain's neurological processes on the mind. Through research and observations, buttressed by the principles I have learnt through my formal training in the natural science discipline of chemistry and later management systems, I have been able to identify some patterns which have guided me in my own decision-making processes, whilst navigating through complex problem-solving situations. In this chapter, I attempt to simplify some key tenets underpinning these patterns, so that I can share with you, in a manner that you too may find some usefulness in applying, as you navigate through your own challenges, being faced with solving complex problems, like we all do, in our daily lives.

Understanding what a system is, while important for learning how to identify the system that you are in, is not enough, especially if you want to build your capacity to solve complex problems or overcome challenges to build resilience. The earlier part of this book focused on identifying when a system exists and how to determine what system you are a part of. You would recall that a system only exists when there is a purpose for it to exist. So, you must, as a start, develop the skillset to identify the purpose that you are a part of fulfilling. To ensure that you and everyone else in the system that you are a part of understand the system's purpose, there needs to be clarity on how this purpose is expressed through a language that is common to all of you.

Always remember, too, that at any one time, you are part of a myriad of systems, each with their own different purposes. However, I believe that all purposes are linked to a single higher universal purpose—which is, after all, the ethos of systems thinking, premised on the basic principle of natural science, which is the connectivity of all energies. Some may attach this higher purpose to a god, several gods, or none at all.

Irrespective of which part of society you belong to, I have written this book with the belief in a higher purpose, and this purpose, simply put, is to sustain the viability of all living systems. Therefore, I would like to believe that every decision I have made in my life has been in support of this higher purpose. In all the sub-systems of this world in which I exist and operate, I always question whether the decision to act would support life or destroy it.

This "higher purpose", however, can only exist if you truly view the world through a lens that enables you to see and believe that all human beings are connected and are existing and operating within systems. Only when you adopt and practice a "thinking-in-systems" approach to life, are you able to make better sense of what is happening in the world around you.

Thinking in Systems

What do I mean by "thinking in systems"? As Linda Booth Sweeney from Harvard Graduate School of Education and John Dennis Sterman from MIT School of Management identified in their 2000 study, to develop the ability to think in systems, you need to develop the capacity to think in a multitude of approaches, which may sometimes be mistaken to be contrary to each other, if not viewed in a holistic manner. This is, incidentally, the first principle to systems thinking. Developing the skill of seeing the "big picture" and understanding how individual parts of the system contribute to its overall function and purpose is of paramount importance. The skill of "holistic thinking" (skill 1) allows you to take a deeper look at the context in which systems operate and how different sub-systems and their components interact to form the whole. But holistic thinking is just the start.

The ability to think dynamically, that is, the ability to see and understand how systems change over time, is just as important. "Dynamic thinking" (skill 2) allows you to recognise patterns and trends in behaviours or variables within your system, whether it is a personal one or an organisational one. It requires, as author Rick Ruben puts it, a "connected detachment" approach, where you consciously detach yourself from the story of life as it is happening. When you do so, you are able to focus on how things are evolving, rather than focusing on just a snapshot based on a specific time limitation within the system.

Closely linked to dynamic thinking is the ability to think and feel comfortable "thinking within a continuum" (skill 3). That is, developing a capacity to recognise that variables within human systems exist on a continuum, rather than in a binary manner. Thinking in a binary manner may be useful, as it makes it easier for the brain to make decisions that way. However, thinking in this manner creates a conundrum in living systems. This is because, in reality, all factors within systems can vary in different degrees, influenced by their context, and it is these variations that impact the overall behaviour of the system. Therefore, continuum thinking is integral to systems thinking.

The ability to think "structurally" and "generically" (skills 4 and 5) are also two key attributes of systems thinking. If you find that you are weak in this area, it would be wise to make a conscious effort to develop this capacity of thinking. Structural and generic thinking will equip you with the ability to identify universal structures or patterns that can be applied to systems operating within different contexts. With structural thinking, you will not just be able to identify the structure of a system, including its underlying components, but you will be better able to understand the interrelationships within your system that shape its behaviour. Equally important is the fact that when you develop the skill of structural thinking, you see beyond individual events taking place within the system, and you are able to recognise the underlying framework and causal relationships within your system.

When you are able to think structurally, I am convinced that the ability to think generically flows naturally, and you will be better able to apply fundamental principles learnt from interacting with one system to another system. As a natural scientist interacting within a myriad of local, regional, and international organisational systems, this craft or skill has come in very handy for me. This is because with generic thinking, you can see how similar dynamics or structures might appear in different situations or industries to produce similar results. This has allowed me to transfer insights gained from one system to another.

Contrary to what many think, being able to think holistically, without the ability to adopt a set of operational thinking skills, does not make a good systems thinker. To think effectively in systems, you must think both at the global level and at the operational level, focusing on the mechanisms and processes that drive change within a system. "Operational thinking" (skill 6) involves understanding how actions, by humans and/or machines, directly cause changes within a system. Operational thinking helps you to simplify processes in a step-by-step manner. This type of thinking is a necessary precursor to thinking in closed loops, - another critical attribute of systems thinking.

The skill of "closed loop thinking" (skill 7) allows you to understand that the components within the system, as well as other systems, are all interconnected through feedback loops, through which energies transfer. The importance of feedback loops was addressed in earlier chapters. At this point, it is important to understand that with closed loop thinking, you can better appreciate the fact that any action within a system can influence other parts of the system and potentially circle back to affect the original action. Developing the ability to recognise feedback loops will help you to understand the cyclical nature of cause and effect, which holds true for all systems.

Notwithstanding the seven skills highlighted above, all of which are needed in order to develop your capacity to think in systems, there is one additional skill, the importance of which cannot be over-emphasised, no matter what industry, sector, or part of the society you are in. This final or eighth skill is the ability to think scientifically. "Scientific thinking" (skill 8) is not an attribute that belongs to only the select few who have studied a scientific discipline. In fact, too often, this term is used in an elitist, exclusive manner, as if only those who identify themselves as scientists have the right to think scientifically. This limited mindset is the cause of the failure of many systems. Once you have a well-functioning human brain, you have the capacity to think scientifically.

By adopting a scientific way of thinking, you can develop a skill that would cause you to act in a manner that is grounded in hypothesis and experimentation to test ideas. More importantly, scientific thinking includes the ability to question assumptions, test variables, and revise mental models based on evidence and outcomes. Surely, this is a skill that cannot only be associated with a select few within our societies. When you adopt a scientific approach to thinking, you better appreciate the fact that experimentation and testing must precede any efforts at systemisation.

Throughout my professional career, my approach has always been to apply scientific thinking, which is a core part of systems thinking, to any efforts focused on systematisation. During this period of over 2.5 decades, I have experienced and witnessed how the failure to do so, before rushing to replicate or scale through systemisation, results in catastrophic outcomes threatening the sustainability of systems. So crucial is systems thinking to the success of any systematisation efforts, that it is necessary to spend some time in this chapter differentiating "systems thinking" from "systemisation".

Systems Thinking vs. Systemisation

For those like me, with what I consider to be an entrepreneurial mindset, we thrive in experimental or innovative spaces without too much structure. We tend to be drained with what some may consider to be mundane issues requiring lots of structure. I know this feeling all too well, especially since the greater part of my professional career has thrown me into administrative roles, directing, and managing. I have learnt, however, to apply systems thinking to all the roles I have played: the experimenter, doer or implementer, manager, mother, wife.

Thinking in systems gives you an opportunity to step back to allow the brain to adopt a "high altitude" view. This stepping back is necessary to discover the purpose of the system. Once discovered, you need to keep a laser focus on this purpose. In other words, any actions you take or behaviour patterns you observe, with systems thinking, you always focus on the "why". Time and energy are two limiting constraints or rules in all systems, and personal ones are no exception. Therefore, by remaining focused on the "why", it becomes easier for you to prioritise your time and energy, focusing it only on the activities and processes that work towards fulfilling the purpose of the system and the related goals and objectives that are set.

On the other hand, although systemisation is a derivative of the word "system", systemisation is only useful for controlling the processes within your system and directing its growth. Systemisation, therefore, involves standardising your processes, which includes establishing rules and constraints within the system. We discussed some of this in the second part of this book. I cannot over-emphasise the importance of ensuring clarity of the rules you establish and ensuring their appropriateness or fitness for purpose to govern the processes within your system, whether it is at an organisational or personal level. While I am not a proponent for excess bureaucracy supported by voluminous documented information, what I do know, however, is that informal rules, which are rules that are not clearly documented and expressed, such as assumptions within the personal system, are as bad as, or even worse than, the absence of any rule at all. Assumptions that have not been verified by factual information can be ultra-limiting on actions to be taken by humans, most times with disastrous outcomes for both personal and organisational systems. With bad rules, it will be challenging to achieve the systemisation necessary to direct and control the growth pathway for your system that is aligned to building resilience.

Experimentation

Be aware of the danger associated with rushing to systemise your processes before testing them. You need to always experiment to see what works first; otherwise, you stand the risk of systemising bad processes—something I have seen quite often. It is a good habit to experiment with different sequences of actions to determine what produces the outputs and outcomes that you desire and, importantly, that are aligned with the overall purpose of your system.

Too often, especially in the developing world, we rush to implement system rules such as standards that have been handed down to us from the developed world. For instance, thousands and even millions are spent on massive projects to help small and medium-sized entities to get certified to "internationally recognised" standards without even questioning whether these standards are a good fit for small businesses operating within the environment that they in. In addition, we rush to benchmark our systems against systems operating in entirely different external and internal contextual environments.

This rush to systemise processes that do not work for our unique systems must be discouraged. While I understand that the need for control is something the human brain is designed to strive for, and perhaps this acts as a key factor that drives the rush to systemisation, we ought to train our brains and our thinking patterns to resist this temptation. Instead, we need to train our brains to think counterintuitively to learn how to feel comfortable in the unknown—the space where experimental research takes place. It is only with experimentation that we can evolve as humans, along a pathway of increasing resilience for our systems.

There are several proven tools and techniques, such as randomised control trials, that could be used to test the processes within your system. However, do this in a projectized manner because you cannot remain in the experimental stages for too long. When you have found the processes that work to achieve the outputs and outcome that you want, you can then move on to integrate them into your system through a programmatic approach.

It is at this point, you are in the systemisation stage, which involves, among other things, standardisation. If you dislike doing the type of work involving systemisation and standardisation—which most people with an entrepreneurial mindset find it difficult to engage in—you can easily outsource it by hiring someone to do it for you, while ensuring that your system's processes are maintained within the rules you have created through your standardization efforts.

Even if you do not enjoy doing this type of work, avoidance of systemisation is not an option. This is because systemisation is a requirement if you want to scale and grow your system and, of course, build resilience into it. While you can hire systems thinkers to do the job, you, as the system's owner or operator, cannot outsource your own systems thinking. This type of thinking is particularly important when evaluating the information received from your system's processes.

The CTS Triad Approach

Systems and systems thinking are so crucial to the survival of your organization, you need to ensure that the decision-making processes within your system, are designed in such a manner to facilitate systems thinking to allow you to maintain control over the trajectory and sustainability of your overall system or the subsystem you are responsible for. Therefore, your entire system must be designed to support not only your systems thinking, but thinking in systems at all levels within your organisational or personal systems. This involves much more than adopting a strategic approach to guide your involvement within your system.

Using the experiences I have gained throughout both my professional and personal life, I have attempted to coin a short three-letter abbreviation that sums up an approach I have found to be holistic and useful in building systems that can be controlled while being sustainable. This abbreviation—CTS—has the following formulaic structure: C_2TS_3 (forgive me for the influence of my chemistry background). For cognitive ease, I have designed CTS to represent a triad of six domains that I have found critical for the application of systems thinking to build resilient systems. These domains, which are reflected in the figure below, are (1) clarity, (2) context, (3) teamwork, (4) strategy, (5) structure, and (6) systems.

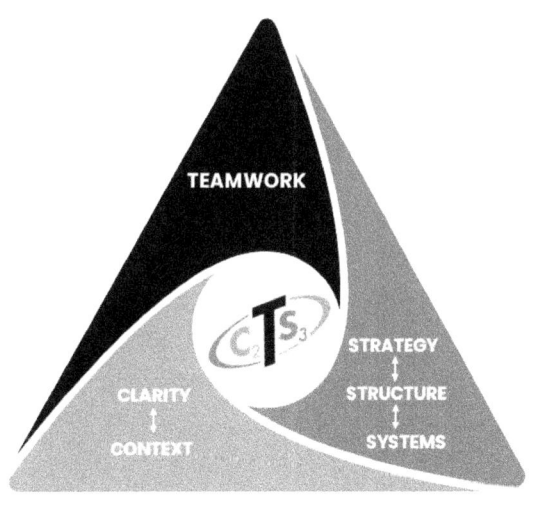

In the CTS triad approach to building sustainable systems, clarity and context are at the base, as it is only when you have clarity on what you want to achieve, whether it is for your personal or organisational system, that you and everyone else within your system can focus on the right thing, in the right direction. This level of focus can then guide the energies to flow in the direction that they need to go, which is towards fulfilment of your goals. Understanding the context within which your system is operating, and the internal context of your system is another critical foundational stage of building resilient systems. A realistic view and deep understanding of your system's internal and external context as it really is—not worse than what it is or illusions of what it ought to be - is crucial to bringing clarity and definition to your system's goals and objectives.

To assist you with achieving the clarity-context dyad foundational step, here are some questions that you may wish to consider answering as a start. These questions could be applied to understanding the context and achieving clarity in any type of system, whether it is personal or organisational.

Clarity

1. What is my/our purpose?
2. What do I/we do?
3. How do I/we do it?
4. How do I/we behave?
5. What is most important to me/us right now?
6. What must I/we do next and who must do it?

Context

1. Where are we at?
2. What is our internal environment and organisational culture like?
3. What is the external environment within which we operate?

Teamwork

Once you have established clarity and you have gained a good contextual understanding of your internal and external context, you move to the next stage. This stage, which addresses the quality of your teamwork, is equally important as the foundational stage, but should only be focused on after you have completed the C_2 dyad. Teamwork stands alone at the apex of the CTS triad for good reason. Too often we forget that we all are working within human systems, and we dismiss or relegate the processes that are focused on dealing with the human psyche and human interactions second to what we consider to be technical matters. In quality management, these processes are referred to as "supporting" processes within the system while the technical activities involved in producing the output that is traded are referred to as "core" processes. This, perhaps, is one of the reasons for this misguided approach that often results in diminishing the importance of such processes in management systems.

Humans are fundamental to both core and supporting processes. Therefore, it is critical to understand humans as the "core" factor of all systems—both personal and organisational. History has taught us that we cannot achieve and manage sustainability in our systems when we do not recognise humans as being the fundamental factor in, and central to our systems. If you want to build and sustain your system, you have no other choice but to put the human being at the centre of your strategy, which the CTS approach does.

Once you have clarity about what you want to achieve, you need to ensure that you have the right people in the right positions within your system to operationalise your strategy and achieve your system's goals. By this, I am referring to the humans who find joy in doing the activities needed at the right stages of the processes within your system.

After choosing the right team, you then need to embed self-respect, or what Harvard Business School refers to in one of its recent publications as "dignity", into your system. You do this by ensuring that your processes are designed in a manner to, among other things, empower the humans who are closest to where the problems are created within the system, to solve these problems when they arise. While strategic and systemic problems are better addressed at higher levels, do not design processes that reserve all the decision-making power to a select few higher up within the hierarchy of your system. Once you have a good structure that supports good decision-making, you will be better able to focus on building effective cohesive teams at and across all levels within your system.

As we saw earlier in this book, a team is a group of humans working together to achieve a common purpose. If there is no common purpose or no common goal attached to this purpose, there is no team. It stands to reason, therefore, that within an organisational system, there will be several different teams at any moment in time. Some teams may be short-lived, associated with a particular project, and may comprise members across all levels within the organizational system. Other teams, however, may be specific to certain levels within the organizational system, and are sustained throughout the lifetime of the system, being tied to its structure.

If you want to prioritise which team to begin working with first, to improve the effectiveness and efficiency in its performance, a reasonable approach would be to start with the leadership team. This is because this is the team that has the authority to make decisions related to the structure of the system. We know that the structure, like any other structure in the architectural or engineering context, is the backbone of your system. If your system's structure is weak, and your decision-making processes are not designed in a manner to respect its integrity and flexibility, your system's sustainability will be compromised. Further, the research literature is replete with evidence that supports the fact that cohesive teams perform the best, and that wherever cohesive teams exist, you are sure to find a sustainable system. My own personal experience has found no other evidence.

Consequently, if you are charged with the responsibility for the performance of a system, a question you should have at the core of your thinking is "How cohesive is our leadership team?" Your leadership team sets the tone of your entire organisational system, so if you are not comfortable with the answer to your question, you ought to prioritise some of your energy to close the gaps identified at that level. You may not have the capacity personally to do so, or you may just not find joy in doing the work needed to close these gaps. Then, get some help. There are many consultants, like ourselves at KMA, who can assist you with the resources needed. These resources can help to systemise the processes related to building and maintaining cohesiveness within your leadership team, and that of all other teams within your organisational system. This is a must for your efforts to deliver meaningful impact before proceeding to the third part of the CTS approach to building resilient systems.

Structure-Strategy-Systems

The final part of the CTS triad approach is itself a triad, focusing on three aspects that should be considered when building resilient systems. The management consulting industry has commercialised some of these aspects to extremes. So much that I have witnessed the resources of companies and families go down the drain trying to copy what others are doing by hiring the biggest names and firms in the field without first taking the prerequisite steps outlined above. That is, to build the capacity of their system to accept and make use of the assistance provided by consultants hired within this space. It baffles me as to why smart people, many of whom I have gained a lot of respect for over the years, continue to make this error, by diving straight into what I have termed the "S triad"—strategy-structure-systems—before doing the prior work needed to make the most of the work done in these areas. I believe that the temptation to delve straight into strategy and systemization continues to arise, perhaps because of constraints associated with time that exist. Time constraints equalise all of us as humans in the universal system, as we all have 24 hours within each day. But we cannot continue like this. I too provide a fee for services in these areas. However, in all my interventions, I try to make a careful effort to enlighten system owners to the dangers of throwing resources into this last part of the CTS sustainability triad, before addressing the primary and secondary areas related to the CT parts of this triad.

Only when CT has been addressed can you focus on the strategy your team can develop to deliver value to the people that your system was created to serve. This strategy will change over time and needs to be constantly reviewed and revised. The frequency in which you and your team do so would depend on the nature of your internal and external context, and the rate at which that context is changing. Whilst process stability is critical to managing change in the direction intended, your leadership team ought to be constantly questioning the relevance and effectiveness of your system's strategy. Moreover, your leadership team should certainly be reviewing your strategy whenever there are major changes to your organizational system's structure brought on by changes within the context your system is operating. This is necessary to determine how you are succeeding and will succeed at delivering value to the people you serve. You may believe you have the best strategy for building and sustaining your system, but if your system fails to deliver value to the people it serves, it will die and, therefore, shall never achieve sustainability.

Once your strategy for delivering value is determined, you need to ensure that the structure of your system is designed and established in a manner to deliver your system's value how you see fit. Be sure to pay attention to the interactions within your system and channels through which information flows. These interactions are an indication of the structure you have in place. The interactions here refer to interactions between humans within your system, whether it is through direct face-to-face contact or through various electronic media.

The final S in the CTS triad approach refers to establishing systems or systemisation. We discussed systemisation earlier in this chapter, and it is not by accident that it is placed in the bottom part, or last, of all the other components in the CTS triad. Systems are dear to my heart, and as mentioned earlier, I have spent the majority of my adult life working in this space. As I write this book, however, it continues to sadden me how sponsors, whether it is through grant or loan financing, continue to pour money down bottomless pits, helping organisations systemise activities based on rules or standards that do not work. This often occurs, because we do this before ensuring that the critical prerequisite components of the CTS model are addressed within the organisational system. To amplify this fundamental error that continues to be made to satisfy demands from buyers and regulators, entities are being incorrectly pushed to systemise processes that have not been piloted or tested within their own systems to demonstrate that they can work in the interest of the system's owners. It is primarily the consequence of experiencing this personal pain of having had to do so myself as an entrepreneur and intimately witnessing the similar pain of other entrepreneurs and leaders of organisational systems whom I have assisted in the past, that has propelled me to write this book.

Now that you have reached this point in the book, I do hope that I have been able to help you avoid this sustainability error. By applying the CTS framework to tackle any problem you experience within your organisational system, I hope I have offered you, among other things, a tool which brings some clarity on the role of systemisation and where it ought to be placed in your strategy to build a resilient system. It is because we are all dealing with human systems, we have no choice but to focus on the human being first, with all its dimensions and varieties of personal systems that each of us brings into the organisation. Centering your efforts first on doing what it takes to make the humans within your system come together and work better for a common purpose, *the big T in the*

CTS model, is a critical prerequisite before any efforts are spent on systemisation. But in order to achieve this prerequisite, understand that you first need clarity on the purpose of your system, *the first C in the CTS model*, and clarity on where you want it to go. If the humans within your system do not have a common understanding of the purpose of the system that they are a part of, how can you expect them to align their personal systems to that of the organisation they are in? This alignment is a necessary ingredient for effective teamwork.

This brings us to the final chapter of the book. By its end, you should understand why the sustainability of a human system can only be achieved if we first address the purpose and needs of the personal systems of the humans operating within it.

CHAPTER 11

Thriving in a Complex World: The Journey Ahead

A bad system will beat a good person every time.
—**W. Edwards Deming**

As I conclude, I reflect on the work of many authors and systems thinkers who have inspired me to get to this juncture and contributed to what has driven me to write this book. Scientist and author Barry Richmond, a well-known leader in the field of systems thinking and systems dynamics, comes to mind. He was the first to be credited with coining the mindset term "systems thinking" in 1987, almost three decades ago. His thoughts, as shown below, expressed as far back as 1991, are ever more applicable in today's world and will continue to be relevant far into the future, particularly in the context of globalisation and artificial intelligence:

> As interdependency increases, we must learn to learn in a new way. It's not good enough simply to get smarter and smarter about our particular "piece of the rock". We

must have a common language and framework for sharing our specialised knowledge, expertise and experience with "local experts" from other parts of the web. We need a systems Esperanto. Only then will we be equipped to act responsibly. In short, interdependency demands Systems Thinking. Without it, the evolutionary trajectory that we've been following since we emerged from the primordial soup will become increasingly less viable.

Since then, there has been tremendous growth in the body of knowledge surrounding systems and systems thinking. Engineer, mathematician, and author W. Edwards Deming, whose philosophy and teachings continue to underpin the globally recognised management system standards developed and published by the International Organization for Standardization (ISO), has had a huge impact on the early development of my career. Deming is most well-known for his work in popularising a model for the theory of knowledge, the Plan-Do-Check-Act, or PDCA cycle. During his lifetime continuously advocated for all policy and decision-makers, which is really, all of us as living human beings, to adopt a systems approach to management. As an American, he is credited for being instrumental to the growth of Japan's economy during the post-World War II period through the industrialisation era. Deming's work has heavily influenced my approach to solving problems in practical life, especially through his book published in 1994 by the Massachusetts Institute of Technology: *The New Economics for Industry, Government, Education*.

Subsequently, the work of Donella H. Meadows, ecologist and author, who has influenced the thinking surrounding sustainable development, has also shaped my thoughts and approach to implementing projects within this space, throughout my consulting career. Meadows's writings on thinking in systems, published over a decade after Deming's work was published, have strengthened my conviction that there simply is no better thinking skillset compared to that of systems thinking especially if building resilience and sustainable development is what we, humans, seek and strive to accomplish.

Perhaps by reading this book, you too are convinced of this, and you have been, or you are now aware that you belong to not only one system, but a myriad of systems which are in other systems on this earth, and by extension, in this universe. These systems and systems of systems, if man-made, are either personal, if its purpose is not shared with anyone else, or organizational, once its purpose is shared.

In the human systems that you belong to, if you are charged with the responsibility of performance and sustainability, you may have also, at this point, come to the realisation that you are not managing people, but what you are actually doing is managing various processes, whether they are decision-making processes, thinking processes, a number of unique personal systems, or just simply sequences of activities. Once you have reached this point of awareness, it means that you are already, consciously or unconsciously, *thinking in systems*.

However, a huge danger exists when you are not able to identify and understand the purpose of the system that you belong to. It is even worse when you realise that you have no other option but to work with other people, whom you may not particularly enjoy being around. But you must work with them anyway to achieve a particular objective or goal, in the absence of clarity on the broader purpose for achieving this objective or goal. If this is the case, if you are unsure of what to do next, a good place to start off is with your personal system. This is because this is the one system that you, and only you, have an agency over. You have the power to steer the destiny of this system. Very often, however, the personal system is the system that is usually the toughest one to work on and to improve. Why is this? I think it is because working on your personal system requires ultimate humility and a breaking down of the ego system. This is the system that is created by the cognitive part of the brain that cares about how the outside world views your personal system. Continuous improvement of your personal system, like any other system, requires you to be constantly in a state of learning. If you are able to be comfortable in this state, you can survive in any system, good or bad.

Sometimes, to survive in a system which has a purpose that is not aligned to your purpose could be quite energy draining. Perhaps mere survival is not what you are aiming for at this stage of your life. You want to do more than survive on this earth. You want to thrive. You want to be able to give more to nourish the growth of other systems you are a part of. The moment you realise the system you are in does not allow you to do that, my advice to you is to make the decision to leave it as soon as you realise its purpose is not aligned with the purpose of your own personal system. When you make that decision, it may take some time to plan your exit from the system, before you can leave. Do your planning diligently and respectfully, especially if you cannot find alignment of purpose with even a sub-system within the overall system you are in. If this is the case, the system is definitely not working for you, but against you, so get out.

Alignment of Purpose within a For-Profit Organisation

Working with several executives and directors of for-profit companies throughout my career, I frequently encounter doubt among executive team members as to whether it is indeed possible to achieve a true common purpose among all team members. This is often because these humans appear to be conflicted or unsure as to whether their actions are driven more by gaining profits than by achieving a meaningful purpose defined by values that are aligned with the values of their personal systems. This dilemma is not surprising because, as you recall, an organisation refers to any group of people coming together for a common purpose.

However, in the context of company law, we need to differentiate between "common purpose" from "common cause". The origin of the very word "company" has its roots in Latin and French, meaning "coming together to share bread", derived from *"com"*, which means "with", and *"panis"*, which means "bread". Therefore, the purpose of company law in a capitalist society is to facilitate the kind of activity that allows for the coming together as a group of people for this common cause or reason.

Distinguish, however, the purpose for using the company law instrument to create an organisational system, from the purpose of the organisational system itself, which was discussed in Chapter 2. The purpose of an organisational system can be fulfilled through varying architectures or structures. For instance, the organisation could be set up as a for-profit or non-profit organisation, a civil society organisation, a partnership of people and entities, or, in its basic form, an association of people. The government and legislature within a society will decide what laws are used to determine the form of organisation that the society recognises and accepts. It stands to reason, however, once the organisation is set up as a for-profit company, the common cause for setting up the organization in this manner, must be, and is always to allow owner stakeholders to share in the profits the company or organization makes.

While the common cause for a group of people coming together to form a for-profit company is to allow for sharing in the profits of the organisation, its organisational system will thrive only if it has a purpose that is aligned to the purpose of the systems within the environment it operates. While all systems, if left unchecked, can disintegrate, the organic purpose of all natural systems, which the business entity is a part of, is to sustain itself. Therefore, the purpose of the business or organisational system that was created in order to generate profits for its owners ought to be to produce a product or service that adds value to the sustainability of the external system that it is a part of, which includes its society.

It is this value that is exchanged or traded for the money from which profits are derived. Therefore, the value of the product or service produced is determined by the extent to which it solves a problem within its natural external environment, or society. This is just simply a

> basic law of natural science, and opposing intentions of no human being can evade this natural law for eternity. Therefore, notwithstanding the adaptability of its organisational system's structure, the sustainability of the company can only be achieved when its governance and management systems allow it to effectively fulfil the purpose of an organisational system that is aligned with the purpose of the systems in its external environment. This environment includes, among other things, the man-made company's legislative system and other societal and natural systems.

By remaining in a bad system, or one that is not aligned to your purpose, your energies will get drained, and this has the potential to kill your spirit for creativity and innovation. Creativity and innovation are so essential for thriving that I believe you ought to use these two factors as a barometer to determine whether the system you are in is working for you or against you. When you leave a system that drains your energy and stifles you to the point where you can no longer create and innovate, never regret moving on and removing yourself from that system's structure. It was not working in your interest anyway. It may turn out that when you are outside of the system you have left, you are better able to contribute to making improvements to that same system.

I have had to make many decisions like this during my life, and often they have been tough. Leaving a system is never easy, many times presenting itself as a feat difficult to overcome, whether or not your departure from the system is initiated by you. However, every time I have made a well-thought decision to get out of any system, whether it was a personal system or professional one, I have experienced remarkable opportunities to allow for the flow of positive energy into my life.

Concluding Summary

I started off this book expressing the view that the quality of energy in the systems you are a part of is everything that matters in life, and this is linked to the fundamentals of thermodynamics. As I conclude this book, I would like to remind you of this force of nature, which dictates how systems evolve towards complexity and unpredictability. Entropy measures how dispersed or spread-out energy is within a system. The higher the entropy, the greater the disorder, and the less energy there is available to do useful work. This makes the case for designing a system with a flexible structure that allows for some order through the use of tools such as standardisation. This is necessary if you want to control the trajectory of your system, and certainly prior to you attempting to implement any improvement initiatives.

It is my hope that this book has adequately used the application of systems thinking to, among other things, demonstrate the critical role of standards and standardisation in stabilising and improving any type of system that you are a part of. The ability of humans within the system to predict well is the hallmark of a sustainable system, guided by systems thinking strategists. However, in the absence of rules such as standards, your system's processes will trend towards more entropy, or a state of low-quality energy. In simple terms, this means that your system will be more disordered. The more entropy there is within a system, the more uncertainty there is about the state of that system, and the more information you will need to describe your system precisely. No matter how brilliant the strategists are or the person you engage in helping you guide your system, efforts on building resilience will be in vain, as it will be too difficult to predict the behaviour of your system over a specified period of time. If you ensure that a systems approach is taken to develop your human system, your chances of not just surviving, but thriving in the environment in which you are operating will be increased tremendously.

Thinking in systems has never failed me, and I know it will not fail you too. I have found that adopting a systems approach to overcoming life's challenges, with all its complex problems, has helped, at least at a minimum, to normalise human emotions that can too often get in the way of logical thinking. As a human being, I have failed many times in this regard, often with not so pleasant outcomes, where my emotions hijack my ability to think in systems. But as a self-proclaimed systems thinker, my personal system continues to evolve day by day, as I allow it to learn from my past mistakes. So, I joyfully continue onwards along this journey of life with its challenges, and I truly hope that the content of this book has made it a little easier for you to do the same.

Acknowledgments

To all the individuals whom I have been led by and had an opportunity to work with while leading and managing various organisational systems and projects over the years, I say a special thank you. Your desire to change "the process" when you knew things weren't going the way they should be set the foundation for writing this book. The world is, indeed, a better place because of people like you, who question and resist maintaining the status quo, just because "this is how it is done!"

To my book production coach, Scott Allan, who has walked along this journey with me, steering me from ideation to realisation—words cannot express my gratitude for the value you have contributed to getting me to this point. My editor, Nancy Pile, who has been so instrumental in helping me transform my impassioned scattered thoughts, in many instances, into a flow that would make it easier for you, the reader, to benefit from, I am truly indebted to you. And to my fellow consulting colleagues, and organizational leaders who have also contributed to the editing process, providing the forwards and formal reviews of this book, - organisations would no doubt gain from the time you have taken to dissect the meaning of some sentences which attempted to express otherwise difficult or complex concepts.

Finally, to my family and friends, some of whom are no longer physically with me, who all stood with me, cheering me on, bearing our long conversations on sometimes abstract matters—your support and love have been my rock, not just along this challenging and rewarding book-writing process, but throughout my life's journey; and will continue to be the lever of my thoughts transformed into words to share with humanity.

About the Author

Alison Foster has had a love for both science and the arts from childhood. She enjoys expressing her passion through written and spoken words, and she uses this passion to spark change within organisations. After years working in leadership and management positions within public and private entities, and even in the businesses which she co-founded and operated in the food and light manufacturing sectors, Alison became frustrated by the continued systemic limitations to growth that she had to overcome. In 2017, she therefore moved on to establish her consulting firm, KMA Consulting, to help organizational leaders solve complex development problems that intersect leadership, governance, management, and operations through a systems approach and systems thinking. With a Ph.D. in Chemistry and Graduate Diploma in Law, coupled with her training in quality and project management, she does this by combining her technical skills and business acumen to help her clients produce high-impact outcomes.

Alison has a deep connection to Saint Lucia and the rest of the English-speaking Caribbean-the region she grew up in and spent most of her professional life. Having been recognised for her contributions to quality and standards within the English-speaking Caribbean, she continues to volunteer her time contributing to national and international standards development, and in other quality infrastructure-related areas.

If you want to learn more about how the application of systems thinking, standards, or any quality-related matter can help you improve your organisation's performance, or if you are interested in having Alison speak to your organisation about these issues, please email her at alison@kma.consulting or visit KMA's website at www.kma.consulting.

www.ingramcontent.com/pod-product-compliance
Lightning Source LLC
Chambersburg PA
CBHW071203160426
43196CB00011B/2184